WHAT WE ACHE FOR

Books by Oriah Mountain Dreamer

THE INVITATION

THE DANCE

THE CALL

OPENING THE INVITATION

WHAT WE ACHE FOR

CREATIVITY AND THE UNFOLDING OF YOUR SOUL

ORIAH MOUNTAIN DREAMER

HarperSanFrancisco
A Division of HarperCollinsPublishers

Grateful acknowledgment is made to the following for permission to quote from their works:

Art & Fear by David Bayles and Ted Orland. The Image Continuum. Copyright © 1993 by David Bayles and Ted Orland. Story included by permission of Ted Orland.

"Fire and Ice" from *The Poetry of Robert Frost* edited by Edward Connery Lathem. Copyright © 1920, 1923, 1969 by Henry Holt and Co., copyright © 1951 by Robert Frost. Reprinted by permission of Henry Holt and Company, LLC.

"The Treasure's Nearness" by Rumi, translated by Coleman Barks in *One-Handed Basket Weaving*. Maypop. Copyright © 1991 by Coleman Barks. Excerpt reprinted by permission of Coleman Barks.

"Things to Think" from *Eating the Honey of Words: New and Selected Poems* by Robert Bly. HarperCollins Publisher Inc. Copyright © 1999 by Robert Bly. Reprinted by permission of publisher.

HarperCollins books may be purchased for educational, business, or sales promotional use. For information please write: Special Markets Department, HarperCollins Publishers, Inc., 10 East 53rd Street, New York, NY 10022.

HarperCollins Web site: http://www.harpercollins.com
HarperCollins®, ☷®, and HarperSanFrancisco™ are
trademarks of HarperCollins Publishers, Inc.

FIRST EDITION
Designed by Joseph Rutt

Library of Congress Cataloging-in-Publication Data is available on request.
ISBN 0–06–001196–3

05 06 07 08 09 RRD(H) 10 9 8 7 6 5 4 3 2 1

For my sons, Brendan and Nathan

May you each be faithful to your own
creative work in the world

CONTENTS

WHAT WE ACHE FOR

one

WHAT WE ACHE FOR

We ache to touch intimately what is real, to find the marriage of meaning and matter in our lives and in the world. We ache to feel and express the fire of being fully alive. When we cultivate and refuse to separate those essential expressions of a human soul—our spirituality, sexuality, and creativity—we feed the fire of our being, we find that place where the soul and the sensuous meet, we unfold. Willing to do our creative work and refusing to separate it from our sexuality or our spirituality, we add a life-sustaining breath to the world.

Yesterday I received news about two people seeking death. One, the elderly mother of a dear friend, declares repeatedly to those at her bedside that she is ready to go, finished with life in a body that seems to be failing by painfully slow incremental steps. Her son, my friend, writes to me of her struggle to leave. Sometimes she verbally rambles, sometimes she lucidly recalls old songs and stories. Mostly she is quiet, waiting. She lies in bed refusing to eat, willing herself to go, spasms running through her limbs from the effort of trying to leave her body, only to find one breath following another and another, continuing against her will.

The other is an old friend who was briefly a lover many years ago, a gifted architect in his late sixties who, despite being well loved by his wife and children as well as many friends, has struggled with depression for years. He disappeared four days ago, and those closest to him fear that he has lost his fight with some inner darkness and has jumped unnoticed from the ferry near his home, has been swallowed by the watery darkness of a January night.

Both bits of news arrived yesterday but only reached me today. Sometimes it takes time for unwelcome information to find a way around the defenses of daily living. This morning I said prayers for the man and the woman and for those who love them and went about my business. But this afternoon, as I drove home from picking up eggs and milk in the village nearby, I noticed the way the crimson light of the setting sun seemed to set the ice-covered trees at the side of the road on fire. Something in this impossible marriage of fire and ice made the muscles of my chest tighten. And these stories of death finally penetrated my body. My skin flashed hot and I was drenched in sweat, and then a bone-deep chill swept through me as I thought of the sought-after deaths: one, the feverish exertion of trying to leave the body; the other, a cold end in black water. The words of the Robert Frost poem "Fire and Ice" ran through my mind.

Some say the world will end in fire,
Some say in ice.
From what I've tasted of desire
I hold with those who favor fire.

But if it had to perish twice,
I think I know enough of hate
To say that for destruction ice
Is also great
And would suffice.

I felt how often we are headed in the wrong direction, fighting the wrong fight, battling with reality and losing. I thought of the aspects of myself that are like this woman and this man: how I strive over and over again to determine something with my will despite all the evidence that it is simply not up to me; how I sometimes mistake surrender for giving up and giving over to that which would rob me of life. To the woman, to the willful aspect of myself, I want to say, "Let go. Let it be as it is. Even this you cannot make happen as you think it should, and if you keep trying, the ease you long for will continue to elude you, and you and those who love you will suffer. It is not *your* life but simply Life, and it will take its own time, follow its own rhythm." To the man, to the part of me that at times, if only for a moment, has felt the icy chill of despair that comes when I realize I am once again not handling well what life has given me, I want to say, "Don't. Don't even allow the thought of throwing it away. Isn't life already too short, over too soon for all that waits to unfold within us? Fight for it. Reach for it, if not for yourself, then for those who come after us, for all of our children. Don't."

I wonder and am somewhat dismayed at how often we hang on where we need to let go and give up where we need to persevere.

I am surprised by how deeply I am touched by these two stories. Connection make us vulnerable to grief and loss even as it offers us the intimacy that heals and sustains us. As I read my friend's letter I think of my own sons and know how much it must mean to this woman to have her son with her as she dies. And I think of my mother and remember that whatever else is true of our relationships with our mothers, they have been the very ground of our physical existence, and so their passing must send a tremor through the emotional earth upon which we stand, must leave us bereft in some fundamental way even when we can anticipate and accept the inevitability of the loss.

Waiting to hear if they have found the body of the man I once knew, I am surprised at how past intimacy makes this loss seem immediate despite the fact that we have had only minimal contact in recent years. I have had other friends die but never one with whom I made love. I don't know why this makes a difference, but it does. Imagining him now, pale and cold from the water, I remember the heat of his hand on my belly as we talked and laughed together in bed. Long-forgotten details return: his skin, soft and salty-sweet; the sound of his breathing blending with the song of the crickets outside the cabin we shared; his habit of rolling toilet paper into earplugs so he could sleep in an inner silence. I wonder and am shaken by the knowledge that despair could win with someone so curious about himself and the world.

As I write I feel both the futility of the words to change what is and how writing, my form of creative work, offers me a way to be with what is. Because who each of us is at the very deepest level of our being, the Sacred Mystery in the form of an individuated soul, is capable of being with it all—the joy and the sorrow, the struggle and the ease, the fire of living and dying, and the ice of despair and desperation. And our essential human nature, our capacity for awareness, for being with what is with an open heart and mind, is cultivated, expressed, and reflected in how we live three aspects of our lives: our spirituality, our sexuality, and our creativity. These three are inseparable expressions of the human soul, that divine life force expressed as a particular human being living in the world. Consciously cultivating and refusing to separate our spirituality, sexuality, and creativity is the way we tend the life of the soul, individually and collectively. It is the way we unfold.

Let me define these three terms as I am using them here. Our *spirituality* is our direct experience of that which is paradoxically both the essence of what we are, the stuff of which everything is made, and that which is larger than us. We can call it God, the Sacred Mystery, the Great Mother, the divine life force, fertile emptiness, clear light awareness, love, beauty, truth. The possibilities are endless. Some experience it through the practices of a religious tradition. For many life's holiness touches them unexpectedly when they attend a birth or sit at the bedside of someone who is leaving this world. Sometimes a direct experience of the sacred comes when we simply bring our full attention to an ordinary moment. Fully present, we experience a presence within and around us, an all-inclusive vastness that is beyond words or thoughts. These moments of being awake to the divine within and around us offer us a sense of purpose and meaning, an appreciation for the wholeness of life even as what we experience in these moments may be impossible to articulate or explain.

I use the term *sexuality* here in the broadest possible way, pointing to the fundamental beauty and fire of physical existence. Years ago I heard a spiritual teacher talk about omnisexuality, the interconnectedness of all life-forms participating in creation, and I wrote an invocation:

I call on a dream of the people that remembers
the power of life-giving moisture,
that recognizes the scent of the sea
where it caresses the shore
in the scent of our sweat
in the salt of our tears
in the slippery wetness that pours
from between the soft thighs of a woman well-loved.

I am referring here to our awareness of the inherent juiciness of life lived in physical form, the infinite variety and vividness of color, taste, scent, sound, and touch in which we participate and from which we draw life. It is life and death, the intimate and inherent linking of flowering and decay that reminds us of the impermanence of all that is physical. Our sexuality is the way we live and appreciate an embodied life, which includes physical ecstasy and agony. It is the orgasmic rush that runs through the limbs when you lie on the forest floor staring up though the towering pines swaying in the wind. It is why a soaring melody is appreciated not simply by the mind, why the opening it creates for touching and being touched by what is sacred and nameless is felt in the body, experienced as a sudden and surprising ache in the chest. It's what makes us want to sit still in the center of the sound of the waves crashing on the shore, move and arch our back in the warm sun after a long winter, savor the taste of food prepared with care and thanksgiving. It is the infinite ways in which we experience and celebrate our passion for this world and the senses through which we taste and nourish the life we are given. Our sexuality includes all the ways we physically experience and are intimate with another, the world, and ourselves.

Our *creativity* is the soul-deep impulse in all human beings to go beyond the perceptions of the senses to the conception of something new. We begin with what is and make something more of it. A piece of wood becomes a beautifully carved and useful piece of furniture. An old way of organizing activities or people or space yields to new innovations. Observations give birth to ideas; words become a poem; sounds become music, light, and color; pigment and canvas become a painting. It is an inherent part of creation itself to produce new forms, and human beings are not separable from creation. I see this creative impulse in the minute front lawns of urban neighborhoods where homeowners spend countless hours carefully arranging stones and plants and concrete statues to create a space that mirrors some hope or dream or story they want the world to notice. I see it in the way advertisers use images of young families, untouched wilderness, and sexually provocative women to sell everything from shampoo to insurance policies. I see it in the games of children, who construct whole new worlds with empty cardboard cartons and illustrate their lives with colored chalk on concrete sidewalks. Human beings are continually creating.

This book is an invitation to participate in a particular type of creative work, creative work that produces things—paintings, stories, poems, music, images, movements—things that can never be completely foreseen because they arise at least in part from the process of doing the work itself. Creative work that makes something new from the paradoxical combination of a focused intent and a willing surrender to something larger than us, creative work that necessitates conscious purpose and expansive receptivity, will, and grace. The politician who constructs a mythology from half-truths in order to win votes, the cosmetics company employee who comes up with innovative names to sell this season's new shades of lipstick and nail polish, the office manager who reorganizes the workplace so tasks can be done more efficiently—each is using his or her creativity. But this is not the creativity I am interested in here, not the creativity I want to invite you to participate in. Each of these cases includes specific desired outcomes, plans to make things that the makers hope will have particular effects upon those who receive the results of their work.

Throughout this book, when I speak of creativity or creative work, I am speaking of work that has unpredictable results and effects, work that is open-ended in how it happens, work that begins with an idea or an intent and proceeds with a surrendering and reshaping of that intent over and over again. I am speaking of creative work that holds surprises, teaches us things we did not know before we began, creative work that changes us, helps us unfold and become who we are at the deepest level of our being. I am talking here about creativity that is inseparable from our spirituality and our sexuality.

Of course, in our culture spirituality, sexuality, and creativity are separated all the time. This separation results in a crippling distortion of all three and frustrates the desire of the essential and sacred life force to know and express its wholeness through a particular human life. When one of the three is separated from the others in our thinking or our actions, something essential is lost and awareness of our inherent wholeness becomes elusive. Spirituality separated from sexuality—from an awareness of and appreciation for our physical life and a material reality alive with sensual detail—loses its fire, the passion that is rooted in the celebration of the beauty and gift of physicality. Separated from creativity—from the deep impulse to take what is and make new connections, to weave together new forms from the strands of daily life—spirituality runs the risk of becoming empty, conditioned rituals that lose their meaning for those who participate in them. Sexuality separated from spirituality—from an awareness of the essential sacred life force energy we are—loses its heart, its connection to meaning and the real intimacy of knowing the other as another manifestation of the same divine presence that lives within you. Sexuality that is separated from creativity becomes mechanical, ritualized, losing its capacity for the intimacy that comes from the mindfulness and spontaneity that creativity requires and provides.

As with spirituality and sexuality, creativity that is separated from the other two faces of the soul loses its vitality, is diminished in its capacity to be a path for the unfolding of the soul. Creativity separated from spirituality is reduced to advertising aimed at manipulating the longings of the soul to sell an idea or product or service. Creativity separated from sexuality loses its aliveness, the sensuality and passion of life rooted in the physical world. It becomes an intellectual exercise that does not touch the heart, stir the blood, or feed the soul.

This book is an invitation to cultivate your essential creative impulse without separating it from your deeply sensual and sacred nature. Of course, cultivating a spirituality that is not separated from the other two expressions of a human soul is also part of the path of unfolding, of becoming who and what you essentially are, of finding joy and offering something to the world. Part of my attraction to the spiritual practices of Native Americans came from an appreciation for how these tribal traditions, unlike many others, do not denigrate the physical, sensual world but see and honor the sacred in the earth and sun, in the creatures of forest and stream. Ceremonies of fasting and praying alone in the wilderness, while adhering to a basic structure, leave room for the creative impulse to manifest in dances and songs and prayers from the heart. And sitting for days beneath the hot desert sun or in the mosquito-infested forest pretty much guarantees you will remain aware of your body, grounded in the world of the senses even as you open to that which is larger. This has been, for me, a path of spirituality that is not separated from my creativity or my sexuality.

Similarly, there are ways to cultivate your sexuality without separating it from your spirituality and creativity. For some this means following a formal path of tantric practices. For many this means consciously being in relationship with another, responding to the creative challenges of finding ever-changing ways to be intimate with each other. When our hearts open, when we really touch each other and allow ourselves to be touched in our lovemaking, in sharing the joys and sorrows of daily living, we experience the sacred in the form of another human being, we awaken to that which is larger than us both.

This book offers a way to cultivate our creativity without separating it from our sexuality and our spirituality. Creative work, at this time, may offer many of us the most accessible road into our wholeness, may be the least problematic way to follow the thread of what we ache for. For many in today's culture, our spirituality and sexuality have been shaped by personal histories of contradiction, confusion, and sometimes blatant exploitation. Our sexuality is often complicated by a collective history of the swing between rigid puritanical mores and hedonistic exploitation. Our spirituality may be distorted by a history of religious practices

that seem to many to be disconnected from daily life or domi-
nated by dogma advocating rigid adherence to one way for all
and intolerance of differences. In contrast, for many of us, our
creativity has been largely neglected. While cultivating our sexuality or spirituality may require years of psychological sorting
and sometimes painful self-examination through therapy or other
guided means, it is possible that we might be able to simply
plunge into creative work. I'm not suggesting that creative work
does not have its own challenges or that it has not been affected
by a culture that narrowly defines art and often schools us as children in producing copycat work. But maybe, just maybe, because
creativity has been so neglected in many of our lives it is a place
where we can approach the life of the soul with a little more ease,
without becoming paralyzed by quite so many demons from our
past buried in the unconscious. Of course, because the three are
not separable, sooner or later the kind of creative work I am discussing here will bring you up against the edges of what is unre-
solved or neglected in your sexuality and spirituality. But hopefully,
the joy, discovery, and momentum of that creative work will keep
you moving deeper into all three.

This book is about learning to focus your intent and engage
your will in order to create while simultaneously learning to let
go, to surrender the process to something larger so that it can
carry you deeper into yourself, your creative work, and the
world. It's about building a life that supports, encourages, and inspires this creative impulse. It's about learning to begin over and
over again because creative work is primarily about beginnings.
On a practical level, no matter what our circumstances or opportunities, at times we must stop doing our creative work to take
care of the business of living—to make a meal, take a child to

school, bathe the dog, or pay the phone bill. This means we must find ways to move around or through or over the internal and external hurdles to start again and again.

But in addition to developing critical practical strategies for repeatedly returning to our creative work, we need to cultivate the attitude that the Buddhists call beginner's mind. When we do creative work, we seek to make something that did not exist before we began, and so we are always entering new territory, forging new pathways. This requires that we be fully present, that we break out of old ways of seeing and leave behind what we think we know. While repetitive tasks like doing the dishes or shoveling snow, if done mindfully, can bring insight and joy, the predictability of their desired outcome leaves minimal room for creativity, means the momentum of the task itself may carry it to completion. But creative work requires that we approach each new project, each new chapter or paragraph, each new musical phrase or time period set aside for writing or painting or sculpting, as a beginning. Of course there are moments, hours, and sometimes even days when creative work flows with a golden ease, when each new phrase or stroke of the brush or movement of the body flows from what has preceded it. But these moments are grace, a gift, something we cannot make happen. Our part is to begin again and again, even when we are reviewing or revising material that is already half-formed. To allow for the surprises, to open to exploring possibilities that we have never before considered, to find the truly creative and unpredictable movement that emerges from within the work, we must always be beginning.

Because creative work is so much about repeated beginnings, several of the following chapters offer strategies for getting started or for bringing ourselves back to the creative work when time and energy are available. The expectation that we need to begin only once, that once we have begun it will automatically get easier to find the time, energy, inspiration, or direction to do our creative work, can bring the work to an abrupt halt. There are no doubt thousands of half-finished novels, paintings, and concertos sitting in dusty closets, testaments to an unwillingness to begin again and again. We have to find new ways to step around the obstacles to starting and prepare ourselves so we are ready and able to do the creative work that calls us, repeatedly stepping toward the unknown and unpredictable as if for the first time.

The stories and songs and images that help us be with the world and ourselves are buried in our daily lives. To see them, to hear what they have to tell us, we must excavate, feeling our way along the edges of a hidden wholeness by painting bold lines on empty canvas, by picking out new melodies on old piano keys, by putting pen to paper. As I began to write today, I started with what is: the stark beauty of sunlight on frozen trees; physical sensations of heat and cold; thoughts and feelings stirred by news of two people; the memory of a poem, the sadness of loss, the recognition of patterns in my life that can cause and have caused suffering. And something inside loosened and accepted and began creating patterns and connections and meaning.

Viktor Frankl, survivor of the Nazi concentration camps, urged us in his book *Man's Search for Meaning* not to ask what the events of our lives mean but to take responsibility for creating meaning from the events of our lives. There is no inherent explicit connection between the two people whose stories have come to me this week beyond my knowing them both. There is certainly no objective link between these stories and the way the sun lights the ice on the trees at the side of the road or Frost's poem about destruction by fire and ice. As I write I do not anticipate the connections the story I am writing will offer to me, I am not thinking about or trying to create something that is entertaining or meaningful for myself or for others. I begin with what is, and I am surprised as I write to feel my way into a wholeness, finding connections that are created as I write, stumbling across insights that remind me of what matters and allow me to simply be with what is. The Danish writer Isak Dinesen wrote, "All suffering is bearable if it is seen as part of a story." Stories, songs, images help us be with what is. We create as a way to be with what is hard and beautiful and unexpected without closing our hearts or pretending something else is true, as a way of easing the suffering that comes when we fight with or try to hang on to what is. And as we create we make it all—the sorrow and the joy, the failed efforts and the places of ease—count. Our stories and images and sounds create, explicate, or point to a deeper meaning that helps us receive, celebrate, and be fed by beauty and bear what is hard. And if the meaning revealed by the process of creating is often more implicit than explicit, still it does not fail to feed us. Because what it feeds is not our minds but our souls, and souls do not need explanations; they need only to touch and sit in the center of the meaning that is enfolded in being.

This is the root of the creative work we do: the desire to intimately touch and share the truth of our lives and our world, to find and follow the sometimes-hidden thread stitching ourselves and our reality into wholeness. Creative work can both reveal and co-create this wholeness from the colors and shapes, textures and tastes of the life that swirls within and around us. This wholeness is what we ache for, the home we fear we have lost and to which we long to return. Susan Vreeland in her novel *The Forest Lover* writes about the life of Canadian painter Emily Carr. She writes of the artist's desire to go "beyond objectivity" to penetrate the heart and spirit of our lives and our world, to see and share what only the soul can see. We create—we write or paint or compose or choreograph, we produce scents and sounds and tastes, images and stories and poems—in order to see who we are, what we value, and why we go on. And we are drawn again and again to create because the surprise of finding an implicit wholeness each time we engage in creative work cultivates our passion for life and brings us joy.

It's what makes us human, this capacity to co-create the truth that sustains us from the stuff of our dreams and our lives. Bruised and battered by the inevitable misfortunes of life, aware of our shortcomings and discouraged by our delusions, distracted by and dissatisfied with the quest to satisfy immediate and temporary needs, we seek redemption in the truth creative work offers us. This truth may disturb or provoke. Sometimes our creative work shouts out our sense of aloneness and isolation and brokenness so we can re-member ourselves and our world as whole, rediscover ourselves as inseparable from each other. But always, even when it mirrors what is hard, even when it disturbs and challenges, the truth of creative work celebrates the unending beauty and connection of life, which never wholly disappears. Over and over again our creative work saves us from forgetting what matters, from our focused productivity and our well-laid plans, from the certainty that we know what is best, that we can make things come out the way we think they should with hard work and harder resolve. Creative work saves us from the smaller self, the self that looks at the world with a tight-lipped, narrow-eyed determination, the self that turns away from softness and life-sustaining idleness, from the silence and stillness where stories and music and images, where necessary wisdom and unearned blessings, find us.

It may seem that I am placing too much of a burden, too many expectations, on what creative work must be or provide. But these are not abstract ideas of what creative work *should* be. They are observations about what the creative work I am speaking of here *is*, what it has provided and continues to provide in my life and in the lives of others I know. These are descriptions not of goals to be achieved by finding and doing our creative work, but of what actually happens when we engage in creative work, of what the process brings to human lives and communities. The form may vary, but the experience of life-sustaining truth and beauty, of discovering meaning and connection, of touching that which is larger than us no matter what we call it, of unfolding our essential nature, is the experience of creative work. Doing creative work allows you to follow the thread of what you ache for into a deeper life, offers you a way to cultivate a life of making love to the world.

USING THIS BOOK TO CULTIVATE YOUR CREATIVE WORK

At the end of each chapter I offer questions for contemplation and practical suggestions for doing creative work, followed by writing exercises. Because my primary way of working creatively is through writing, the particular examples and practical suggestions are sometimes geared to the writing process. However, I have discovered from observing and talking with friends who are composers, photographers, musicians, performing artists, filmmakers, and painters that despite the particular demands and requirements of specific forms of creative work, what is required to begin and continue, the pitfalls and struggles, the rewards and satisfactions are more similar than different. And so the suggestions for doing creative work offered here can be adapted to any medium of expression. Some writing exercises are geared to helping you uncover your own creative motivations and methods. Others are intended simply as warm-ups, ways to get your creative juices flowing. Hopefully the creative movement begun there can be taken into further writing or any other medium of expression. When doing the writing exercises, decide on a time limit for each exercise, and commit to writing steadily for whatever time you set, starting and completing the phrase or answering the question over and over until the time has expired. Warm-up periods can be as short as five minutes or as long as twenty.

I offer ideas for contemplation by posing questions that begin with *What if* . . . Prefacing ideas with this casual-sounding phrase is a way of slipping past our resistance to considering perspectives that might threaten our carefully constructed sense of self or our preconceived notions of reality. Using the phrase *what if* hopefully increases our chances of seeing what previously we might have missed or dismissed. It provides an opportunity to shift into an attitude of wondering, into a process of open inquiry. You may want to write in response to the questions. They can also be contemplated by simply sitting with them or carrying them with you as you walk through your day, noticing how your inner and outer worlds respond to the inquiry held in your consciousness. In any case, I suggest that each time you go to the questions you first spend a moment settling into the here and now, slowing down, taking a few conscious breaths, and allowing yourself to be truly present before reading and being with the questions.

The practical suggestions offered are intended to help you find your way to begin, continue, bring to completion, and share your creative work. I encourage you to experiment with and pay attention to what works and does not work for you. If my insights and suggestions help you to write, paint, compose, or engage in whatever form of creative work appeals to you more than you have in the past, then use them. If they do not, ignore them and try something else. Ultimately the path of creative endeavor is particular to each person who walks it, although we can learn a great deal from each other and ease the way with shared stories. May what I offer here enable the creative process that is life itself to unfold through the shape of the particular man or woman you are.

FOR CONTEMPLATION

- What if consciously cultivating your spirituality, sexuality, and creativity is the way you tend the life of the soul, individually and collectively? How are you tending these three in your life right now? Where are they integrated? Where are they separated?

WRITING EXERCISES

- Complete each of the following phrases repeatedly for a set period of time. Replace the word *write* with one appropriate to your medium of creative expression (*paint, compose, dance, play music,* etc.):

> *When I write I feel . . .*
>
> *When I write I see . . .*
>
> *When I write I discover . . .*
>
> *I ache for . . .*

- Answer the question: Why do you write (or paint or compose or dance, etc.)?

- Repeatedly complete each phrase in the time you have designated for this exercise:

> *I don't know . . .*
>
> *I don't know how . . .*
>
> *I don't know if . . .*
>
> *I can forgive . . .*
>
> *I can't forgive . . .*
>
> *There's always enough . . .*
>
> *There's never enough . . .*

- Write a story that begins

> *The dumbest thing I ever . . .* (use other superlatives: smartest, silliest, hardest, easiest, strangest).

two

BEGINNINGS

O f all the stages of the creative process, beginning is, for me, the most difficult. It is in the hours just before I sit down at my computer or pick up my pen and open my journal that I experience the greatest resistance to writing. I discover all kinds of other things that suddenly have to be done: setting up that long-postponed appointment to have my eyes examined; making airline reservations for a trip more than six months away; rearranging the tea towel drawer. The list is endless. After years of finding this is so, I do not expect it to change. I accept that I may always find within myself some inexplicable reluctance to begin a process I fundamentally find rewarding. I do not take this as an indication that I shouldn't be writing or that it is not a useful way for me contribute to the world or learn about life. The rewards of the creative process, the many reasons I write and the great joy it brings me, are too consistent to let the difficulties of beginning stop me from writing.

I will share with you here a bit of what I have learned about why I resist beginning the creative process. But you should know that all my honest self-examination has done little to change the strange feeling of wanting to avoid writing that wells up within me just before I begin. Understanding the resistance has done little to make beginning easier, although it has helped me devise ways of slipping around or walking through this sticking point that could otherwise stop the process before it started. Although there is sometimes a reluctance to do my daily journaling—something I will discuss in chapter 6—I experience the greatest resistance to writing when I am beginning a particular piece, writing a new poem or short story or starting a new book. As the day and time I have set aside to begin approaches, I feel a strange but familiar dread, a slight tension in my chest, a barely perceptible agitation in my arms and legs. If I sit with this sense of uneasiness, I discover a wide range of not particularly unique or fascinating fears: the fear that I have nothing worthwhile to say; the fear that this time I will not be able to find the end of the thread that will take me into an effortless flow of words; the fear that the writing will simply be bad—unclear, uninspired, awkward, tedious. But beneath all these is the fear that the creative process will affect me in some unpredictable way, requiring changes in my life that will be at best uncomfortable and at worst truly risky. This latter fear is probably the strongest, and it has a basis in experience. Creative work, because it cannot be separated from our spirituality, inevitably connects us to that which is larger than us, and experiencing the sacred center of life can create a shift in perspective, can bring new insights and understandings that demand something of us.

Over the years, as part of my spiritual practice of studying within an intertribal shamanic tradition, I have gone out on vision quests, times of praying and fasting alone in the wilderness. Following traditional guidelines for ceremony, some quests last two to three days and nights while others last for much longer periods. My longest quest was twenty-two days and nights. Most of the time I head out into the wilderness thinking I know why I am going, holding in mind a central question for which I am seeking guidance. And I always have hopes and expectations about how the quest will go, ideas about what I might find or what changes the experience might bring into my life.

And I am wrong almost every time. Over and over again I have returned from quests surprised and not infrequently frightened by what I have learned and what this learning will require of me. On my first vision quest I realized that my physical health, which had been devastated by years of chronic fatigue syndrome, required that I shift the focus of my life to feeding my own spiritual fires. So, despite a lack of physical strength and material resources, I began to find ways to seriously study shamanic ceremonies and teachings. Returning from my second quest, I left my marriage and began life as a single mother of two small boys. After my third quest I quit my job and began to teach full-time the spiritual practices I was learning, living on whatever came from the classes and gatherings I held in my home. You can see why I might begin to approach vision questing with some trepidation. Even when the changes that came from these times of deep introspection and contemplative prayer were more internal than external, they were no less traumatic to my carefully constructed sense of self. Ultimately it was a vision quest that signaled the time to leave the teacher with whom I had been studying, a difficult and painful decision that led to the reclaiming of my spiritual authority and taking responsibility for my life.

Although I still spend periods of time praying and fasting alone in the wilderness, I can see that writing, my creative work, has become my most consistent way of opening to the wisdom. This is probably why I feel resistance at the beginning of the creative process. I really do not know where it will lead on the page or in my life. Finishing a book about letting all action come from a place of a stillness within, I had to sit still and be with my tiredness, my desire for deep rest and a changing sense of direction in my life. When I did this, when I followed where the writing led, I discovered that I needed to stop the teaching, public speaking, and workshop facilitation I had been doing for thirty years. Following the impulse that came from the stillness I had found while writing, I sent out a newsletter announcing that, with the exception of brief book tours arranged by my publisher, I would be taking an indefinite sabbatical from public speaking as of my fiftieth birthday in September of 2004. I do not know where this time of emptiness will lead. I imagine writing more, trying my hand at fiction, learning more about poetry, considering playwriting. I hope for new insights into how I might return to speaking and teaching in a way that is less physically taxing and offers something to those who come. But I do not know if any of this will happen. I don't know if the impulse to move more deeply into writing or back into speaking and teaching will come from the stillness or if I will simply sit and stare at a wall. In the face of financial fears for an unknown future and with the dissolving of external roles to which I have often anchored my sense of self, I do not know if I will be able to even find the stillness. But writing about the still center changed me, as all creative endeavors change us, and the cost of pretending not to know what the writing has revealed this time—that it is time to stop and see what comes out of the emptiness—would be too high to consider.

Change, even when it ultimately leads to living from deeper and more consistent contact with the still center of our being, is never easy. Someone, after reading a story I had written about what we long for at the deepest level of our being, said to me, "Writing for you must be what going to war is like for men. Every moment, life and death." I do not pretend that sitting at a desk even comes close to the terror of finding oneself in the midst of life-threatening physical battles. But when we enter the creative process fully, we put our carefully developed sense of self, and all that we have put in place in the hopes of preserving that sense of self, on the line. And that can feel like life and death. Any creative process entered into fully and honestly can and often will lead to a transformation of the one who enters it willingly because it involves engaging with something larger than us, touching a truth deeper than those we have previously known or allowed ourselves to acknowledge. Afterward we see and know differently, even if we cannot articulate exactly how, and this difference, this change in perception, requires that we act differently in our lives and in the world. When we bring all of who we are to our creative work, our souls unfold, consciousness is cultivated, and we cannot help but co-create the meaning that comes from touching truth. This is how our spirituality is intimately intertwined with our creativity. The questions to ask yourself as you write or paint or compose are *Is that really true? Is that something I know or imagine or hope to be true? Is that the whole truth? Am I hedging at all? What am I holding back? What don't I want to write or paint or explore? What am I refusing to risk?*

Jewish theologian and philosopher Martin Buber, in his book *I and Thou,* describes art as the result of a relationship between the artist and what he calls a *form,* what could be described as an archetypal force, the divine mystery in the shape of a particular potentiality that wants to be manifest in a creative work—a story, an image, a musical phrase. Buber warns that we are changed from our experience of touching and engaging with this force that is larger than us, even as we change it in the process of creating an actual material work from the encounter. When we faithfully serve the creative impulse that comes from our relationship with this form without holding any part of ourselves back, something is created that offers receptive beholders their own experience of that same form, their own encounter with a particular face of the Great Mystery. Holding back, wanting to control where the process will take us, Buber warns, will result in being broken or in breaking the gift we are offered.

My experience of writing is that I am indeed engaged with something beyond my small self, something that changes me and requires that I live true to any transformation that takes place. This is what makes creative work vital and exciting. This is what can make it frightening. This is what makes our creative work capable of offering something to others. Images, stories, and ideas that come from an unfettered encounter with that which is larger affect both the author and the beholder of the work deeply. It is knowledge of and a deep appreciation for this potential that can sometimes help me to carve out time and energy for writing when other demands or self-doubt would stop me in my tracks. But if we focus on how our creative work can affect ourselves or others, if we begin to see the process as Potentially Profound or ourselves as Messengers of the Mystery, we are just as likely to become paralyzed by self-importance or frozen from fear. To begin writing, to start any creative work, we paradoxically must take seriously the life we have been given while at the same time taking ourselves—our hopes and aspirations, our fantasies and our fears—with the proverbial grain of salt.

Life is a blessing. For some of us it holds the gift—the coincidence of time, energy, resources, and inclination—that offers us the opportunity to act on the basic human impulse to create. This incredible opportunity, whether it takes the form of a full-time occupation or much-loved unpaid labor, is not to be taken lightly. It is a gift, grace, and because it is an unearned blessing we cannot tell what may come from our efforts to honor the process, what effects the work we do will have in our lives or the world. That is not our business. Our business is to honor the gift, do the work, and give ourselves to it completely while keeping sight of our human fears about failure and fantasies about achievement. In all honesty, given the number of neurotic fears and distracting dramas my mind plays out, it is a wonder I write anything at all. And if you create because you think that your creative work will give you some immortality, think again. Even a Bach or a Beethoven, whose work may well be shared and revered for hundreds of years, is less than a blip on the time line of creation, and very few of us are a Bach or Beethoven. Human beings as a species, so far, take up less than a few minutes on the evolutionary curve of millennia. I am not suggesting that what we do—whether or not we engage in creative work when the opportunity presents itself—does not matter. It is why we are here. We, no more and no less than every other life-form in the universe, are manifestations of Life itself multiplying and creating infinite forms over and over again. So the next time you find yourself unable to begin, paralyzed by an inner voice that says, "Who am I to write or compose or paint or dance?" you might try responding with "Who am I not to create? Who am I to refuse to express the inherent creative impulse of Life lived in and through this particular human form?"

So we begin our creative work knowing the profound potential of the process while simultaneously acknowledging our bumbling blindness, inadequate skills, and vast ignorance of where we are going. But we are willing, and that is the necessary prerequisite. However, willingness alone is often not sufficient. First, there may be a few obstacles to be removed. I often have some idea of how I want my life to be when I begin writing, an ideal of when would be a good time to start a new book: a time when my house is immaculately clean and my closets have been reorganized; a time when the mailing list is completely updated and all correspondence has been answered; a time when I have in front of me weeks, preferably months, of uninterrupted days, days when no one will need anything from me, when no one will be expecting me to return a phone call or answer an e-mail, to negotiate a contract or help them with their homework; time when there are no distractions, when my husband and I are living together in seamless harmony and my sons are happy and content, managing their lives without needing anything more than a weekly telephone conversation during which I provide small sounds of encouragement.

As you can imagine, if I waited until these and a thousand other imagined ideal conditions were in place, I would simply never get started. And not only do I have ideals about how my life, my home, my family, and the world should be in order to begin, I have a number of ideas about how *I* should be when starting the process. I want to begin when I am fired up with new ideas, ready to dive into the subject matter at hand with enthusiasm, feeling my fingers cannot type fast enough to keep up with the flow of ideas, the appropriate stories coming with effortless ease. The truth is, I often do experience moments of unfettered enthusiasm, whole hours of effortless flow in the process of writing, but rarely right at the very beginning. The time I have available for writing is much more likely to be shaped by things other than immediate enthusiasm for the process and has been carved out between facilitating a weekend workshop and helping my son revise his résumé, squeezed in between attending a friend's birthday celebration and painting my bedroom. Most of the time I need to write at the time that is designated for writing whether or not I feel like it, or the process simply will not get under way.

We have to let go of our ideas about ideal conditions for beginning if we are going to start. How we do this is really quite simple, although not necessarily easy. There is a time to acknowledge resistance and just keep walking into the thing we are resisting, and this is one of those times. Step over the overflowing laundry basket, leave the breakfast dishes piled in the sink, ignore the flashing light that tells you there are telephone messages or e-mails waiting to be answered, and cling to your commitment to begin on this day. If you want to do creative work, you will have to accept that at least some of the time there will be housework left undone and social occasions missed.

Of course, being willing to begin, we now need a place to start. Coming up to a new project, we usually have ideas about either the form or the content. Perhaps a melody line has been running through your head, or you noticed the way the light creates color around the pond at the end of the day, or you have been thinking about a feeling or thought or event upon which you want to base a piece of creative work. Often I begin writing because a story or image or idea, which invariably seemed at the moment of inception like a brilliant and inspired place to start, has presented itself. I arrive at the time set aside to begin, sometimes many days after having the original idea, surprisingly attached to starting with this idea and often alarmingly disconnected from it. Life has been happening in the meantime and has put me in a very different frame of mind and heart than I was when the idea first came to me. Now I do not want to write about this idea or story or image. Sometimes the notes I scribbled in my journal about this seemingly brilliant idea are illegible or simply don't make sense.

Just as there are times to acknowledge resistance and keep on walking through it, there are other times when it is more effective to sneak around the resistance, to go at the process sideways. The critical thing is that you begin to do the creative work, get and keep your pen moving across the page or your brush sweeping paint across the canvas or your fingers moving on the keyboard. In order to do this, in order to create anything that has enough juice to keep you or the eventual beholder of your work engaged, you have to begin where you are. On the day I was to start writing this book, I pulled out and looked at the notes I had been compiling on the idea of creativity as the means and ends of what we ache for. But I was distracted, not in the place where the ideas I knew I wanted to include in the first chapter really caught my attention or imagination. News of the imminent deaths of two people I knew were preoccupying my thoughts and coloring the way I saw everything from the trees at the side of the road to my own life struggles. So that's where I started. And because creative work is both shaped by and a reflection of the underlying interconnectedness of all life, starting where I was led effortlessly into the ideas about creativity that had been percolating in my mind for months.

Sometimes the piece we do at the beginning of a larger project may not make its way into the completed work. Artists often make dozens of preliminary sketches no one ever sees. Often what I write as I begin does not end up in a book. These pieces disappear into the black hole of the computer file I have labeled "Unused Bits." Sometimes what we create at the beginning of a project may contribute to a later piece of the whole. We eventually discover that we have written chapter 10 first or developed a scene that does not appear until the third act of the play. There is no rule that you have to begin working with what will ultimately become the beginning of the piece. And sometimes, in ways that delight me, in ways that I could not have imagined beforehand, the material I write when I begin where I am ends up right there at the start of the book, bringing me (and hopefully the reader) into the only place where the creative process can happen: here and now.

Sometimes there is no pressing story or preoccupying thought or feeling that demands attention, nothing that says, "Start here." Sometimes I come to the computer or my journal and I am not particularly inspired by where I had planned to begin or a pull to write about something else. On these days I use the countless writing exercises I have accumulated from facilitating writing groups over the years to get my hand moving. Some of these warm-ups are exercises I have invented. Some are from others' workshops or books, although I admit that after using and modifying them repeatedly, I rarely remember their source. Others have been suggested by members of writing groups I have facilitated.

Most are a combination of available resource materials, personal invention, and others' suggestions. I will talk more in chapter 7 about the particular use of these warm-up exercises within a group doing creative work, but for now let's just focus on how they can be used to step around resistance to beginning and into the creative flow.

A warm-up is generally a specific, structured suggestion. Years ago, when I was facilitating painting workshops, we discovered many ways to begin. Sometimes we painted for short time periods (five to ten minutes) with specific instructions. Sometimes we painted with only our hands. Sometimes we painted from the feeling evoked by listening to brief contrasting pieces of music. Sometimes we limited ourselves to two colors or moved around the room adding to the painting of the one before us until the circle had composed ten paintings collectively. My younger son, Nathan, has done dozens of group and solo warm-ups while studying drama: sounding, moving, improvising according to structured suggestions, usually for short periods of time. Warm-ups are intended to simply get us moving in the medium we have chosen. There are a number of writing warm-ups at the end of each of the chapters in this book. Warm-ups are a low-risk way to begin the creative process because they are arbitrary, often set up by someone else and so relatively free from the expectation that you will produce something brilliantly profound or inspiring. When we lower our expectations and simply follow the directions for a specified length of time, it is easier to slide around fears about beginning and simply start. And sometimes, perhaps because of the lack of expectations, perhaps because of the attitude that a warm-up doesn't really "matter" or isn't "real" writing or painting or acting, sometimes because we are willing to just have fun with an exercise, the end of a thread that leads to deeper work presents itself.

This was true for me when I wrote the prose poem "The Invitation." Months before writing this poem, I had attended a writing workshop with poet David Whyte. David gave us a writing exercise based on his poem "Self-Portrait" from his book *Fire in the Earth.* He asked us to write repeatedly using and completing the phrases "It doesn't interest me . . ." and "I want to know . . ." I had great fun with the exercise and used it repeatedly on my own to get started at writing and to discover what mattered to me beneath surface concerns. So when I returned home from a party late one night in the spring of 1994 and sat down to write about my dissatisfaction with the completely normal but superficial level of social interaction I had experienced, I used David's writing exercise to begin writing about my thoughts and feelings. The result was a prose poem that eventually, without my knowledge, traveled around the world via the World Wide Web after I'd shared it with a few friends and students.

Sometimes a warm-up turns out to be more than a warm-up. Sometimes a warm-up is a way to find the end of the thread of something you want to create but cannot put your finger on, a way to scratch an elusive tickle at the back of your mind. I have often used a particular image to open my imagination and begin writing: with my eyes closed, I picture the still surface of a deep, dark pond and take a few breaths, relaxing my body. Then, without any rush, I imagine a slender arm coming out of the depths of the pond with an object in its hand, and I begin to write about the object held in the hand that emerges from the pond. Once, many years ago, the hand held an iron, and I wrote a story I had heard about the early days of my parents' marriage when my father had asked my mother not to have the ironing board up when he came home from work. The story opened me to an unexpected tenderness toward my parents as young adults in a new marriage and offered me surprising insights on what my mother had taught me about relationships.

Years ago, at a writing retreat I was facilitating, I offered this exercise as a warm-up and we began to write. Because we had the luxury of the extended time provided by a weeklong residential retreat, we decided to write for an hour, each of us using the image of an object in the hand rising from the water as often as needed to begin again and again. At the end of the hour Mary, who had clearly been struggling to keep writing, looked at me and said with a nasty note in her voice, "I bet you were a straight-A student!" I laughed and asked her what had happened for her during the warm-up.

"Nothing!" she said. "I kept getting crazy images that didn't go anywhere, and then I would look up and see you over there writing like a maniac, probably writing the great Canadian novel from one instant image, and I wondered what the hell I was doing here!"

I smiled and read her what I had written. Over and over, as I'd sat with my eyes closed, I'd seen a succession of images: a sword, a feather, a man with golden hair. . . . I'd written about the images one by one, letting my imagination wander until it hit a dead end, until I found myself reaching to make connections, bored with what I was writing. My number-one rule for warm-ups—in fact for all creative work—is: If you are boring yourself, stop. Stop and start again somewhere else. Stop midsentence, midbrushstroke, midscene, midsong. There is no rule that says you have to complete a sentence, an image, a thought before you stop. And you can pretty much assume that if you are bored with what you are producing, it is not going anywhere. Stopping, of course, means beginning again. Often when I find my enthusiasm for the writing I have just begun dwindling, when I find myself impatient and bored with what I am putting on the page, it's because I have gotten myself caught in offering background information or writing a preamble to the main event. I am circling around the place I want to be. So I stop and begin again, jumping directly into the thing I want to say, the place in the story that is the juiciest, the image that glows brightest in my imagination. The perspective needed to discern if preambles or background explanations are needed to help readers comprehend is generally more accessible after the essential story is told. You can always go back and add a note of introduction, but getting caught in preambles as you begin can too easily abort the whole process.

As I read aloud what I'd had scribbled in my journal during the first hour of that writing retreat, Mary's eyes widened. She had assumed, because I had kept writing steadily for the hour, that I had created a long and seamless story. In fact, what I had from my hour were pages of false starts, beginnings that fizzled quickly and went nowhere. And then, literally in the last five minutes of the hour, I had caught the end of a thread that held the color of life out to me. Starting with the image of a gold ring held in the hand that rose from the dark waters of my imagination, I had begun the story of helping my sons prepare for their father's (my ex-husband's) wedding day. It was the end of a thread I followed in a later writing session at the retreat, writing a story that ended up being part of a larger piece.

As with every aspect of the creative process, the important part is to keep going. And the truth is that any creative process contains many beginnings. Each day I sit down again to resume the writing, every time I initiate a new chapter or a new story, I find myself beginning again. Sometimes I encounter the resistance of the first day all over again, nod my acknowledgment to the voices that fear some truth will be revealed that will change everything, and just keep working. Sometimes I turn my face away and search for a way to slip past their wary vigilance unseen and unnoticed. Sometimes when I need to start again, I get stuck. When this happens I may need to shift perspective to see where I am going. Sometimes I move, take my laptop to a different place or leave my computer and pick up my pen. The slower, more tactile process of writing by hand sometimes eases me into the beginning, gives me a chance to follow some impulse of the body into finding the words I seek, switching back to the computer once the flow has resumed and I find my hand weary and unable to keep up with the words that are coming. Similarly, I know artists who, when they do not know how to proceed with the painting or sculpture they are working on, move to a different spot and begin to sketch. Because the creative impulse cannot be separated from our sexuality, our physicality, it sometimes helps to move our body when we are stuck—to go for a walk or a run or to simply open ourselves to spontaneous movement, moving or dancing where we are until we can begin again.

When creative projects cannot be completed in one sitting, we may want to try to end at a place where we know and are excited about what comes next in the hopes that tomorrow's beginning will be easier. And sometimes it works. Sometimes we are able to effortlessly pick up the trail and follow the markers left the day before, going deeper into the work. But on other days, we find that something has shifted and we are not where we were when we stopped yesterday. The trail has grown cold. We have to begin again from the present moment. Creative work weaves a wholeness from all the new beginnings, just as our lives weave a wholeness from each new day. To engage in any creative process, to live each day fully, we have to find our way back to the willingness to begin again and again.

FOR CONTEMPLATION

- What if, in order to create anything that has enough juice to keep you or the eventual beholder of the work going, you have to begin where you are right now?

- What if doing creative work leads to unpredictable changes in how you see yourself, how you live your life, how you respond to the world?

BEGINNING

- Imagine your worst fear: you will write meaningless, boring drivel; you will create a masterpiece. Complete the phrase,

    I am afraid that if I write (paint, compose, etc.) . . .

After each imagined horror write,
    Knowing this, I will write (paint, compose, etc.) anyway.

- Set aside a specific time to begin. (Monday at 6 a.m.)

- Mark it on your calendar as you would any important commitment, and when the time comes, put yourself in

front of your computer or easel or keyboard, behind your
camera, or in your studio, and begin.

- Jot down ideas for warm-ups, short, arbitrarily structured
  exercises that use the medium of your expression. These
  are intended not to produce profound work but simply to
  get you going. Keep a list and add to it.

- If what you thought you were going to work on does not
  appeal to you, begin anyway. Use a warm-up exercise, a
  low-risk way of beginning. Write a letter, paint ten paintings in ten minutes, compose a jingle that's a personal ad
  for a mate, a home, a job.

- Keep working for the whole of the time you have set aside
  even if you never get beyond doing warm-up exercises.
  Stop if you are boring yourself and switch to a different
  warm-up or to something that draws your attention in this
  moment.

WRITING EXERCISES

- Complete the following phrases repeatedly:

  *Sometimes (or right now) I don't want to write (or paint, or
  compose, etc.) because . . .*

  *In order to write (or paint or compose) the way I want to, I
  need . . .*

- Remember a beginning. Write a story that starts with one
  of the following:

The first time I met . . .

The first time I drove . . .

The first time I made love . . .

The first time I was truly alone . . .

The first time I got a job . . .

(or use some other first)

- Open a book (dictionary, fiction, nonfiction) at random, let your finger pick out a phrase or sentence, and use it as the start of seven to ten minutes of writing. If you come to completion or a dead end before the time is up, open the book and randomly pick another phrase. Just keep writing.

- Do the same thing with a magazine, but focus on a picture, a visual image.

- Sit and close your eyes and take several deep calming breaths. Clear your mind, and let your attention follow your inhale and exhale. Imagine yourself beside a deep, dark pool of water. Suddenly you see a hand emerging from the depths and holding an object out to you. See the object. Write (or paint, compose, dance, etc.) about it. If you come to completion before the time is up, return to the image of the pond and see the hand with another object.

three

THE SEDUCTION
OF THE ARTIST

I once attended a movement workshop in which participants were instructed to spread out in a large dance studio and mark a place on the hardwood floor with pieces of colored tape. My spot was marked with a small, fluorescent pink *X*. The instructor told us to think of the spot we had marked on the floor as our place of inspiration, the only place in the room where we were allowed to inhale. When the music began we could move anywhere in the room by any means we chose—walking, rolling, running, crawling, dancing—but we had to return to the spot we had marked on the floor to take our next breath. At first I stayed very close to my spot, afraid I might not be able to find or get back to it when I needed to take a breath. I was surprised to feel how strongly the suggestion that we could inhale only at our spot affected me physically. Clearly, no one was stopping me from breathing elsewhere, but I could feel my chest tighten and my pulse quicken as I moved away from the spot. But gradually, as I repeated the exercise and became more familiar with where my spot was, more certain I could reach it when I needed to, I began to relax and venture farther and farther into the room.

I learned a great deal from this small exercise. No matter how far we roam, we always need to return to the places, people, and practices from which we draw inspiration and vitality so we can go out into the world again. We must inhale to exhale, must receive what sustains us if we are to have anything to give. And the more practice we have at finding and recognizing what feeds us, the easier it becomes to venture away from the familiar and into unknown territory. In our creative work we seek not only those places where we can rest and renew so we will have the physical and mental energy to do the work, but also those places where we find the inspiration that makes our fingers itch to pick up a pen or paintbrush or instrument. Long before we sit down to get started, our choices have stacked the deck for or against the possibility of actually engaging in creative work.

Doing creative work is a lot like giving birth. And producing a healthy baby (good book, painting, sculpture, song, film, etc.) is possible only if we have engaged in the process that makes conception possible in the first place. We have to find ways of getting ourselves in the mood. I will tell you here what kinds of things make me receptive to the urge to create, inspire me to want to write, offer me ideas and ways of seeing that give rise to stories I want to pursue on the page. But as with physical lovemaking, you will have to experiment and see what works for you. Some find that satin sheets and violin concertos soften their hearts and warm their bodies. Others find themselves responding with greater ardor to black leather and heavy metal guitar riffs. Still others crave unanticipated variety. There are, of course, those glorious moments when a rush of heat takes us unexpectedly and carries us from clearing the dirty dishes off the table into a passionate embrace on the table. Similarly, the creative impulse may take us suddenly from standing around at the annual workplace Christmas party feeling bored to frantically writing on cocktail napkins words that will become the opening paragraph of a magnificent novel. But most of the time even such seemingly sudden bursts of eagerness for physical lovemaking or creative work are preceded by the deliberate cultivation of a connection with our inner fires, by the ongoing seduction of the lover or artist within.

If we do not consistently stir our creative impulses, we may find ourselves arriving at the time we have set aside to do creative work feeling a lack of desire to do anything more than stare at the computer screen or blank canvas. And there are an infinite numbers of things—surfing the Web, answering e-mails, wandering off to start making dinner or put our CDs in alphabetical order—readily available to fill that void.

Very few have the opportunity to do their creative work full-time, and even those who are so blessed have generally come to this after years of composing after the kids are in bed, taking photographs during their lunch hour break, or writing on the commuter train on the way home at the end of a very long day. These small snippets of time and opportunity may not be ideal for creative work, but sometimes they are all that is available on a regular basis. And because our busy lives tend to keep us in perpetual motion, we may not be willing or able to dive into lovemaking or creative work when occasional periods of time for either become available. Many couples with small children have few opportunities and little energy for lovemaking. Once in a while a couple will find themselves with a rare half hour alone, or a generous grandparent may offer to take the children for an entire night. But if the sensual heart connection between the couple has not been consistently and deliberately cultivated and maintained, they may find themselves spending those precious private moments arguing about who really is more tired or working separately in the futile hope of catching up on long-neglected chores instead of making love or curling up in each other's arms for a nap. Similarly, even if we diligently set aside a regular time—an hour, a half day, a weekend, or longer periodic retreats—to do our creative work, we will not be able to use that time fruitfully unless we have consistently fed our connection to that which stirs the creative pot and inspires us to want to write or paint, dance or compose.

Cultivating a consistent connection to the flow of our creative ardor in the midst of a busy life, like finding ways to remember yourself and your partner as sexual, sensual beings when neither of you has had an uninterrupted night's sleep in the past two years, generally does not happen without deliberate planning. This means letting go of the myth of spontaneity, the illusion that if you were really in a loving relationship you would fall into each other's arms with passionate abandon every time the opportunity presented itself. It means confronting the fantasy that if you were really a writer you would find yourself effortlessly clicking away at the keyboard for every second of the designated hour squeezed between a business meeting and picking the kids up from school, even if you have not had a second to take a conscious breath since the hour you set aside for writing last week. A useful idea in Julia Cameron's *The Artist's Way* is that of the "artist's date," a planned weekly excursion to attend some kind of arts event in your community. It could be a play or a movie, an art exhibit, dance performance, or musical concert. It may be a night of spoken-word poetry at the open mike in your local pub or a lavish production of Puccini's *Madame Butterfly*.

I am always a little skeptical when someone tells me they want to be a writer and then tells me they don't read. Growing up, I was one of those kids who smuggled a flashlight into my bed so I could read beneath my covers late into the night, stopping only when my eyelids refused to stay open. It was reading the book *The Stone Angel* by author Margaret Laurence when I was ten years old that made me want to write. It was the first time I felt the magic that could be created with words, saw how words could breathe meaning into the inner and outer worlds of a seemingly ordinary life.

Writers have an ongoing love affair with words. We're fascinated by the way words can capture a moment, an image, a concept, or a feeling, how they can open the heart and eyes to seeing what was not there the moment before, how they can co-create something instantly recognized as true. That's why we choose to express our creative impulse in writing. So writers need to pay attention to words if they are going to find them ready and waiting when the opportunity to write arises. Writers need to read to learn how to write, to inspire the writing impulse, and to remember the sheer joy they find in words. They need to read writing they love, writing they wish they had written, writing that stirs them and reminds them of the power of words.

Similarly, each form of creative work holds for its author a love affair with the ingredients of his or her chosen medium. Painters love paint, color, shape, images. Carvers love the grain in the wood, the movement hidden in solid stone. Composers love sounds, melodies, harmonies, and rhythms. Filmmakers, playwrights, and actors love stories, voice, and movement. Photographers love light and shadow, texture and color. And all artists, whatever their medium, need to take themselves regularly to the places where the work they want to do is done by others, letting it inspire and stir them.

Of course it is possible to use reading or visiting art galleries or watching films, like anything else, to avoid doing your own creative work. When I am actively engaged in writing a book, I read only at the end of the day, and I am careful not to read books of the same genre as the one I am writing. I do this both to avoid unconsciously picking up a tone and rhythm that is not my own and to dissuade myself from believing that I am working on my book when I am simply reading someone else's. When I am writing creative nonfiction, I read fiction and poetry and analytical texts. When I am not working on something specific, I read pretty much anything I can get my hands on, and I read every day.

Often, I feel I am actively engaged in a conversation with an author whose words move me, writing questions and comments in the margins of a book or writing entire imaginary dialogues in my journal when a piece of writing, sometimes just a phrase or an image, captures my attention or takes my breath away. Reading Coleman Barks's translation of "The Treasure's Nearness" by thirteenth-century Sufi poet Rumi, I feel the final lines like a soft blow to my solar plexus:

> *The more skill you use, the farther you'll be*
> *from what your deepest love wants.*

I recognize some devastating truth in these words, a truth I want to understand, a truth to which I feel a need to respond. So I pick up my journal and begin to write the questions it stirs:

What is it that my deepest love wants? What is the skill, the hard work, I put my faith in to bring this deepest love into my life? Why won't this work? What would work instead? I "talk" to Rumi on the page, and he responds in this imaginary conversation, sometimes with re-membered snippets of other poems, sometimes with questions or comments that my pen pulls from the ethers of the imaginary realm or collective unconscious.

Work that has been successful in keeping the creative impulse intertwined with the sexual and spiritual aspects of life always makes me want to write. Recently I read Ann-Marie MacDonald's book *As the Crow Flies*. Her vivid descriptions of family life in the early sixties stirred my ardor for writing that is rooted in the sensory details of daily life, evoked my own memories from that same time: the smell of wet wool, children's sweat and day-old bologna sandwiches in the cloakroom at the back of my third-grade classroom; the way we knew things in our bodies—in the tightening of our stomachs or the strange bubbling flutter in our chests—when we were too young to have the vocabulary to re-veal what we knew or to feel we had a right to ask questions; the excitement of trying new items from the never-ending procession of the always new and improved things on the market—Pop-Tarts, color televisions, ballpoint pens, French fries served with cold root beer in thick frosted mugs.

Other books, even as they offer images embedded in the sen-sual nature of the world, inspire primarily in the way they eluci-date previously unseen connections that run through our lives, the way the author's creativity is inseparable from his or her spir-ituality. Susan Griffin's books *Woman and Nature: The Roaring In-side Her* and *A Chorus of Stones: The Private Life of War* are two that repeatedly reinspire me to remember the mysterious process whereby writing, or any other creative endeavor, can reveal the wholeness of life and the meaning embedded in interwoven colors and sounds and stories.

As important as it is to observe and note what gets you in the mood to create, it is equally important to know what distances you from your creative imagination, what creates a dullness or tiredness that simply does not feel up to the task, and to consistently avoid these things. The artistic expressions I find the most effective for stirring my creative impulses are the ones that require something of me, the ones that leave gaps to be filled in by the imagination. And so I find radio shows like the weekly storytelling of Stewart McLean on CBC's *Vinyl Cafe* offer me more than most television programs, which tend to leave little or nothing to the imagination. Watching the play *The Far Side of the Moon* by Robert Lepage, I feel the delight of seeing how the imagination can build a world around a skillfully offered suggestion. In this one-man show a round window on the back wall of the set morphs from a spaceship porthole into a washing machine door and later a metaphorical birth passage. An ironing board used in a conventional manner is later flipped over to become first a bicycle and then a convincing snowmobile skimming over the frozen landscape.

Getting in the mood to do our own creative work may mean deliberately cultivating our connection to a particular expression of someone else's work. You may hear a piece of music on the radio and feel a tug, the impulse to write or paint or move from the feeling or mood the music evokes. You may not have any specific idea of what you want to create, only that you are drawn to find the words, color, or movement that holds the same texture and color as this music. Find a recording of the music and play it while you are washing the kitchen floor, taking a bath, or driving to the grocery store. Listen to it carefully, notice how your body feels as the music washes over you. Through repeatedly listening to the music, you will carve a pathway into the place where a particular impulse to write or paint or move can find you, playing the music again when you have the time and space to do your creative work.

Sometimes we may feel intimidated about approaching a form of creative expression we know nothing about. We may have been prejudiced by something from our past, a moment when a teacher suggested that we were just not smart enough to fully comprehend or appreciate some form of creative expression. The beauty of being an adult is that we will not be graded on our art appreciation, will not be asked to explain the artist's intent or what a play or piece of music means. We do this for ourselves, and if something leaves us cold we can simply get up and walk away. And if we can remember that we are adults, that we will not be evaluated for our opinions or reactions, we may be able to confront old prejudices and insecurities, may be able to simply be with some form of creative expression that previously seemed intimidating or incomprehensible and receive from it the inspiration and energy to do our own creative work.

Many years ago, with no background or experience in visual art, I found galleries to be intimidating places. I wondered, Should I move steadily through the images presented or skip those that did not appeal to me? Should I read carefully the notes posted on the wall or in the program, or should I let my response to the images be unmitigated with information on the artist and his or her intentions? Then I read a piece by Jeanette Winterson in *Art Objects* in which she urges the beholders of art to pick a piece of creative work that appeals to them (even if they can't articulate why) and simply stay with it, come into relationship with it. Something in me loosened as I found permission to simply behold one piece of art, to stay with it for an hour or two. I was relieved to find I did not need to *do* anything, could simply be with the piece and see what it said to me, what I said to it, what I could see over time if I simply brought my full attention to the artist's work. What a relief to go to the Metropolitan Museum of Art when visiting New York and allow myself, if I wanted to, to visit only one painting in the midst of such an overwhelming presentation of art! Winterson's advice freed me to be with art as I might be with a good poem or a close friend—intimately.

Since my sons were six and nine years old, I have taken them each summer to watch Shakespearean plays at the Stratford Festival in southwestern Ontario, hoping to acclimatize their ears to the beauty of spoken poetry before they were taught to fear its unfamiliar rhythm. In the same spirit I often go outside and read poetry aloud to the creatures of the forest surrounding my home. Reading poetry silently to oneself, like reading Shakespearean dialogue silently from the page, rarely does it justice. Although there are musicians who can look at a musical score and hear the music in their minds, most of us need to at least pick out the notes on a piano if we are to get a sense of the melody. Similarly, poetry is more easily made accessible to the heart when it is brought to life by the sound of the human voice. Often, after giving a talk in which I have recited some of my favorite poems, I am approached by audience members who express their amazement at how the poems touched them. They recall the fear of poetry that has been with them since earlier school days when poems were treated as dead things to be dissected and analyzed.

They had come to believe they were just too dense to find the meaning buried in the words on the page. They found a new way of being with a form of creative expression they had not connected with before.

In addition to opening to your creative impulse by partaking of others' work, you might let your creative work be fertilized by becoming a neophyte participant in a form of creative expression other than the one you usually use. Working in a medium that is not your forte means you are less likely to fall into grandiose expectations, unfruitful comparisons, or paralyzing envy. My friends Peter and Diana are deeply committed to their creative work. Peter is a wonderful photographer and writer, and Diana uses photographs and her computer skills to create powerful paintings. Recently they both started doing what they are calling "glue art," projects that use anything and everything—old computer parts, shells, beads, fabric, sparkles, flowerpots, mannequin heads, old wigs—to create weird and wonderful sculptures. Neither of them thinks they are going to get rich doing glue art. In fact, I think they might fall over if someone asked to buy one. But they are having great fun with their hot-glue guns in part because they don't expect to create Great Art. As in the case of writing warm-ups mentioned in chapter 2, creative juices flow when expectations can be lowered and there is little or no attachment to results. I do some painting with acrylics and play the piano, both badly and just for fun. And some days, tickled by a musical phrase that my fingers finally manage to play effortlessly, or drawn to the vivid color I have painted in a bold slash across the page, I feel the impulse to write coming to find me.

Sometimes hearing about another's creative process is what inspires me to do my own work. Orson Scott Card, whose books of science fiction and fantasy (*Ender's Game, Speaker for the Dead,* and *Xenocide* are just a few) feed my love of good stories, writes eloquently in many of the prefaces to his books about where the ideas for his stories come from and how they become woven into novels. His stories of how the writing takes place have served to reinforce my faith in the creative process. His candidly talks about the many false starts, the abandoned plot ideas or characters that get picked up later and developed within new stories, the story lines that reach a baffling dead end, where they sit for years until a friend or colleague unexpectedly asks a question about a long-forgotten character or situation, opening a whole new direction. His descriptions of the process deepen my conviction that no creative work is ever wasted, whether or not it leads to an immediately completed work that is shared, and make it easier for me to keep writing.

The creative path is often a circuitous route that can be mapped only in hindsight. It requires faith in the process itself if we are to continue. Diana Meredith, co-creator of the aforementioned glue art, is an artist who paints with her computer. Her finished pieces of this innovative work are very powerful, but equally inspiring is the Web site where she shares each stage of the creative process that goes into finished pieces. It is here I can see a painting being built, layer upon layer, changing directions, bringing surprises, unfolding. Similarly, I am awed and encouraged by my son's accounts of the collective efforts, the weeks of rehearsal, the development of characters, the acting and directorial choices that go into a theater piece. Finding out about the behind-the-scenes processes that go into another's creative endeavors can help us appreciate our own efforts and find the faith and fortitude to continue.

Continuing the creative process today is much easier than it once was. Writing today in a country where paper and ink are cheap, plentiful, and easily accessible, where computers and reliable electrical power eliminate the need to rewrite by hand or even type pages of text every time I want to rearrange paragraphs or chapters, I am stirred by the commitment required by those who came before, those who had to make their ink and paper or acquire a tanned hide as a precious writing surface before they could begin. When I read in Sophy Burnham's *For Writers Only* of the months Michelangelo spent working with a crew to cut by hand and transport by horse and cart a single piece of marble needed for a sculpture, only to have the commission canceled, I am inspired to go to my desk and begin writing even when doing so requires the herculean task of lowering my housekeeping standards. I read in Tillie Olsen's book *Silences* of a woman writing pages by hand on the ironing board in her kitchen amid dirty dishes and half-prepared meals and am grateful for the wonders of permanent-press fabrics, dishwashers, and microwave ovens.

I find within myself a sense of responsibility that does not feel like a burden but a blessing bestowed simply because I was born in this time and this place. I feel responsible to those with little or no opportunity for creative expression: to the men and women who are never given a chance to learn how to read or write; to the women without choices who die well before they reach my age because they gave birth to more babies than their bodies could sustain and buried more children than their hearts could bear; to those whose daily existence is completely preoccupied with the struggle to survive and care for their children amid poverty or violence. The privilege of living here and now comes with the responsibility to co-create what is life sustaining from the opportunity we have been given to do our creative work.

I think of the writers who inspire me, both living and dead, as my creative ancestors, the holders of a lineage of which I am a fledgling member. What I am talking about is claiming the creative lineage you want to learn from, those whose work you want to honor as that which keeps your creative juices flowing, as that which you dream of continuing and expanding upon in your own small way. When I read the work of those I claim as my forefathers and foremothers in the art of writing, I consciously invoke the spirit of their creative impulse and ask to feel the presence and experience of their work supporting my own. The list includes mystics and mythmakers: the ancient Sufi poets Rumi and Hafiz; poet-philosophers and theologians Goethe and Meister Eckhart; modern spiritual teachers like Jack Kornfield, Toni Packer, Pema Chödrön, Jon Kabat-Zinn, and the Dalai Lama; modern poets Mary Oliver, William B. Yeats, Michael Ondaatje, Joy Harjo, Jane Kenyon, Anna Akhmatova; storytellers like Margaret Laurence, Isabel Allende, Marion Zimmer Bradley, Tad Williams, Rohinton Mistry, Ursula Le Guin, Umberto Eco, Anne Lamott, Guy Gavriel Kay, and Barbara Kingsolver. The list is endless and ever expanding.

Claiming a creative lineage is a daring act. Who am I to claim, even in my own mind, to be part of a lineage of mystics, poets, and storytellers from many different cultures and times? Nobody. Just one more lover of words, one more small human being seeking to touch what is sacred and celebrate the gift of being alive by bringing my imagination to what this sensual world offers us. But isn't that who all of our foremother and forefathers, all the writers and artists, musicians and composers, known and unknown, were?

Books, movies, plays, painting, sculpture, poetry, dance, music—
you have to experiment, to see what stirs your creative juices.
Sometimes I think it is the exposure to expressions of others' creativity that ensures I am in the mood, willing and able to access
the impulse to do my creative work when the time and place are
available. Or perhaps it is simply that tending that part of our
lives signals to inner and outer forces that we are willing and
committed to the process, makes sure we are in the flow of creativity within and around us. If Buber is right and all art comes
from an interaction with something that is larger than us, something that is an archetypal force or form waiting in potentiality to
be expressed through our creative choices, then perhaps we are
not only seducing our own creative impulse but also signaling to
that unknowable force that we are willing to engage. As we seduce the artist within, our sexuality, the impulse to create felt in
the body as physical desire, weds our spirituality, that direct experience of something larger than us. And our creative work is
shaped, colored, and moved forward.

FOR CONTEMPLATION

- What if no creative work is ever wasted, even when we
  cannot see where it will lead, even if it is never publicly
  shared or acknowledged?

- What if, in the midst of a busy life, we must deliberately
  and diligently cultivate our imagination and our creative
  impulse, seduce the artist within, not waiting for it to
  spontaneously arise?

GETTING IN THE MOOD

- Over the course of a couple of weeks, notice and begin to list your places of inspiration—the people, settings, and activities that stimulate your imagination and leave you feeling in the mood and energized to do creative work.

- Notice and list also those people, places, or activities that dull the edge of your creative impulse and leave you feeling like you have no energy or inclination to engage in the creative process.

- Now, consider how much time and energy (including but not limited to financial expenditures) you spend on the items included on each list.

- Consider: Is there a need for change? Be specific. Make a plan. How will you include something that you know stimulates your creative impulses this week? Is there a way to make sure that setting up times for creative stimulation are included regularly in every week? What's the easiest way to make this happen? Buying season tickets or a membership at the art museum? Getting a library card? Arranging to meet a friend at a particular time and place? Which of these is practical (easiest, affordable) for you?

- What might you need to let go of to make room for this in your life? Are you willing?

WRITING EXERCISES

- Who are the Grandmothers and Grandfathers of your tribe? What is the creative lineage you claim as your own? Who are the men and women whose work touches and mirrors your own inner knowing? List them. Write a letter to them calling upon them, making your pledge to them to do your best to carry on their tradition of creative work. Ask for their help.

Pick one of them, and write three questions you would like to ask this person if you could. Now write the person's responses to these questions.

- Complete each phrase repeatedly for the time allocated:

    I will never be . . .

    I belong to . . .

- Complete the phrase *I love . . .* in reference to a person, a place, a story.

- Write in response to the request, *Tell me a story about a person or place you love.*

four

LEARNING TO SEE

Wisdom I was in my final year of high school, I wrote a short story that my English teacher, Mrs. Kemp, thought was fit for publication. With my permission she submitted it to a publisher who was collecting short stories, and although it turned out to be too late to be included in the collection, she urged me to write more stories and show them to her. Flattered by her support and tempted to believe if only for one fleeting moment that I could write, I tried. But it didn't work. The stories I wrote were flat and contrived. Hoping and trying to write interesting stories and assuming, as most teenagers living in small towns do, that nothing interesting had ever happened in my life, I reached too far beyond my own experience and wrote stories that lacked the sensory details that might have brought them to life. Discouraged, I decided that if I was ever going to write it would have to be when I was older, after something—anything—had happened in my life that would provide me with stories worth reading.

The truth is I didn't really need to wait for something to happen. Things were already happening. Life was being lived within and around me all the time. What I needed was the ability to see what was happening, the ability to bring my imagination to that life and to create from it the stories I wanted to tell. I don't mean to suggest that people should write only about things they have experienced directly. I would not want to put that limitation on imagination. In Michael Cunningham's book *The Hours,* I read vivid accounts of the inner lives of three women, written by a man. And despite the fact that the lives of these women are in many ways different from my own or the author's, the authenticity of the realities depicted takes my breath away, pulls me in to the inner and outer worlds of the characters that live on the page. Clearly, neither historical fiction or futuristic novels would be possible if we were to confine our creative work to the material of our own lives. However, what I am suggesting is that engaging, creative work that truly lives for the receptive beholder is sparked by and draws upon the details of the inner and outer realities of our lives and the world.

This is what I mean when I say our sexuality—our sensual physical life—is inseparable from our creativity. And these are both completely intertwined with our spirituality. Spirit and matter are two views of the same reality. As the physicist Ernst Mach said, "The universe is not twice given." If this is so, the creative life force that seeks manifestation in the work we do—Buber's *form,* that which is larger, with which we engage when we create—speaks to us through the sensory details of our inner and outer worlds. We find the material by learning to be aware in new and expansive ways, by allowing our perceptions, those of the present moment and those stored in our memories, to fuel our imaginations. When we are aware of life within and around us, we are flooded with the raw materials of creative work, perceptions that spark the imagination and details that bring the work to life for others. To create we have to learn to see.

Years ago, overhearing me read a story I'd written about a retreat I had facilitated, a friend said, "It's amazing to hear you read that story. It wasn't until partway through that I realized that I'd actually been there for the events you were describing. I didn't even recognize the story at first."

I immediately felt defensive, accused of fabricating parts of the story or misrepresenting what had happened in some way. "Did I say anything that was untrue?" I asked.

He laughed. "No, that's not it. All the facts were there as they had happened. But you saw a story, something with a beginning, a middle, and an end where I would have just seen a series of events."

He was right, and he was as mystified by what I had done as I had been when looking at a painting by Monet in the Metropolitan Museum of Art in New York. I'd stood before the painting in awe of the multitude of colors Monet had painted in the water of a lake. How could he see like that? How did he see all those colors where most of us see so much less? Monet had created art, an image of wholeness and beauty from the light and color he saw in the water. I, far less impressively, had created a story, a wholeness that had its own inherent meaning and completeness from the thread of connection I had seen in a series of events. That's what we do when we create: we take the world as it is offered to our imagination and we make something more of it, something particular that simply would not be without the addition of our consciousness, something that is connected to the larger life force that runs through everything and that is revealed in the sensory details of the physical world. We express our spirituality, our sexuality, and our creativity and see the face of our soul.

Quantum physics suggests the possibility that we are always co-creating the world from a vast sea of potentiality with the addition of our consciousness. According to the Heisenberg Uncertainty Principle, certain subatomic particles such as photons can be experimentally demonstrated to be either particles or waves depending upon the question an observer seeks to answer. If the observer wants to know where the photon is and sets up an experiment to give him or her this data, the photon will behave as a particle and its position can be determined. If, on the other hand, the experimenter wants to know the photon's momentum, a different experiment is done, the photon behaves as a wave, and its momentum can be established. We cannot determine both the location and momentum of a single photon because as soon as we answer one question the photon has become either a wave or a particle, and you cannot determine a wave's position or a particle's momentum. Until an observer brings his or her consciousness to the photon by setting up a specific way of observing it, we could say the photon is simultaneously both wave and particle, that it exists as both in potentiality until the act of observation collapses it into one or the other singularity. Clearly, something, some kind of packet of energy—a photon—is there. As far as we can tell, it exists with or without an observer. But when it is observed in a certain way, the photon ceases to be potentially both wave and particle and becomes in reality one or the other.

In creative work we add our consciousness to what the world offers to us in order to create new stories, images, and sounds that reveal insights, patterns, and truths we may not have seen before. But to do this we have to be able to get our conditioned responses—the belief, for instance, that water should be depicted in paintings as blue—out of the way so that we can see the fullness of the world within and around us. This is harder to do than we might think. From our earliest childhood we have been taught to see in mutually agreed-upon ways. When my older son, Brendan, was in junior kindergarten, his teacher asked his father and me to come in for an interview to discuss Brendan's perfunctory participation in classroom art projects. Mystified, I packed up several pieces of artwork Brendan had done at home and went to the school. The teacher, clearly frustrated with Brendan, showed us picture after picture that he had drawn in school in response to directions she had given the class. When she'd asked the students to draw a picture of the place they lived, he had drawn the outline of a black box with a red triangle on top. Beside the "house" was a green ball atop the brown stick of a tree trunk. A yellow ball in the upper corner was presumably the sun. All the pictures he had drawn at school had clearly been done quickly and without much thought or care. I spread out one of the pictures from home on the teacher's desk. Every inch of the paper to the edges and corners was crowded with images at different angles, in a multitude of colors and with little or no regard for the laws of gravity. There were kings with gold crowns at the top of the page and huge birds flying through the air beneath them surrounded by multicolored forests and strange animals and people engaged in different activities.

The teacher stared in disbelief at the contrast. "Well," she said at last, "clearly Brendan does not find my directions inspiring." I refrained from asking why she felt compelled to direct four-year-olds in creative expression. Was it important to evaluate them on their willingness to comply with another's way of seeing? Why not just turn them loose with paint and crayons and paper? She looked at Brendan's father and me with real concern. "Brendan," she stated emphatically, "is not going to do well in the public school system. He is not a team player. He does not care enough about what others think about what he does." His father and I, not as free of the desire to have others think well of us, suppressed our smiles.

She was right. Brendan did not do well in the public school system. Living by the rhythm of your inner drummer, or by the map of your creative imagination in whatever form that takes, holds its own challenges. But perhaps it is easier to deal with the consequences of being out of step with the world around you than it is to find the creative impulse when you only see the world in narrow, preconceived ways. And external authority—the voice of the parent or teacher or media source that tells us how to see—is not the only or the most tenacious authority we have to shake off in order to see things in a variety of ways and let our imaginations respond unfettered. Recently, reading spiritual teacher Krishnamurti's admonishments not to surrender to the very normal human desire for certainty and security by acquiescing to any external authority's notion of how things are, I was feeling pretty self-congratulatory. Having been through the fire of studying with and then leaving a spiritual teacher, having reached the age of fifty and finding myself less inclined to court others' approval, I was feeling relatively free of the influence of external authority on my ability to see the world around me.

But as I read further I discovered Krishnamurti asking for something more, asking us to see what is without relying on the authority of our own experience. For the first time I considered how, despite my resistance to external authority, I often allow the authority of my experience—that which has come before—to shape what I see in this moment, including how I remember the past. Of course, experience can be useful. When I get in my car to drive on icy roads, it's important to remember what I learned from last year's unexpected and abrupt trip into the roadside ditch. But when I am observing the world and myself, when I want to take in the raw material of creativity, my past experience conditions my mind and often dictates what I see and how I see it, narrowing the range of material to which I can bring my imagination in order to create stories or poems or images. Giving my experience authority over my seeing, I do not expect to see beauty at the garbage dump and so may miss the way the piles of snow-filled tires make black-and-white patterns of light and shadow. My mind, conditioned by the authority of my experience of growing up in a small town, does not expect to see a story in my weekly visit to the local post office, and so I may miss really seeing the woman who hands me stamps and parcels, may not even notice the exchange we have or consider the meaning I might have found in a story about our encounter.

One of the easiest and most enjoyable ways to become aware of your conditioned way of seeing, to open to new perceptions, is to spend time with people who see things differently than you do. Most of us spend time with people who share our worldview, people who think and see in similar ways. It gives us comfort to have the authority of our experience reinforced by another's experience. Being with those who have had different experiences and so see differently not only opens us to new perceptions but also helps us become aware of our habitual blinders.

Years ago a talented and innovative composer came to study shamanic ceremonies with me. During one retreat I facilitated, she took a tape recorder down into the gorge that ran through the property where we were staying and recorded the sound of the water rushing past the rocks and echoing off the cliffs on either side of the river. These sounds became the inspiration for and part of her later compositions involving electronic music combined with the sound of the human voice. Watching her work and learning to appreciate her music, I started to listen differently, to move past expectations about what I would hear in different settings, to suspend instant judgments about which sounds were pleasant or musical, to perceive a much wider range of sounds. I began to notice relationships between sounds, began to imagine a layered wholeness in the sounds of our inner and outer worlds.

I am fortunate to live with someone whose ways of seeing are very different from my own. While this can sometimes lead to lively debate and points of contention, it is also presents ongoing opportunities to expand my ways of seeing. My husband, Jeff, is a talented photographer. Often he takes pictures of things I don't even see: the rich colors and textures of peeling paint and rusting metal on a shed wall; the delicate lace of melting ice set against the dark wet wood of the back deck framed by sun-sculpted snow; shadows in doorways or windows that hint of other worlds. Also, where I am a mystic, Jeff is a scientist. I meditate, read poetry, and study metaphysics; Jeff designs computer hardware, builds telescopes, and is an avid astronomer. We have different areas of expertise, but because the world is inherently interconnected, when we can set aside our preconceived notions about both the world and our abilities to comprehend what is unfamiliar, we offer each other new ways of seeing and imagining the world we share.

Recently, thinking about time, I asked Jeff to explain to me how atomic clocks work. After he explained cesium resonances to me, we began to talk about our culture's preoccupation with measuring time precisely and the adjustments made to calendars over the centuries. Jeff told me about the advent of the Gregorian calendar in 1582. As the new calendar was instituted, ten days had to be dropped in order to bring the dates into alignment with astronomical data. There was apparently considerable unrest about this at the time as the poor and uneducated feared the rich and powerful were trying to rob them of ten days of their lives. This got my imagination going: What if you really did have to wipe out ten days of your life? What ten days would you never be willing to surrender? What ten days would you be happy to miss? And what if a gap really did exist in time? What would happen to the continuity of cause and effect? What would happen to all the things that would have or could have happened in those ten days and the things they would have caused? Possible elements of science fiction and fantasy stories began to percolate in my imagination.

Sometimes it just takes a shift in perspective to help us see the world a little differently, to spark the imagination in new ways. Young children are particularly good at teaching us how to see past our conditioning, how to let what we are offered stir the imaginative mind. They simply don't have much experience. Everything is new to them. The stones in the driveway, the difference in the texture and taste of the round and the square sides of the crust on the bread, the way the cat washes herself—these are all fascinating when you are five and can lead to endless imaginative speculation. I remember preparing dinner one night when Brendan was about six years old. He was sitting at the kitchen table, silently and slowly opening and closing his mouth. I looked at him and raised my eyebrows in query. "If we could unhinge our jaw, do you think we could fit a bowling ball into our mouths?" he asked thoughtfully. I just shook my head and laughed, delighted with the seemingly senseless but fascinating meandering of the imaginative mind.

Recently CBC radio reported that a western Canadian university decided to use the relatively unfettered perspective and imaginations of children to teach engineering students how to think more creatively. They paired engineering students with boys and girls in grade three, asking the eight-year-olds to imagine what kind of furniture they would like to have in their rooms. Then it was up to the budding engineers to find a way of making the furniture the children imagined. Apparently a hover-chair and a bunk bed on giant wheels were two of the projects that delighted both those who had conceived and those who had designed and built them.

We have to become aware of and set aside our conditioned ways of perceiving in order to hear the rising symphony in the rush of the river, to see the beauty in a bit of ice, to find the story beneath a series of events, to imagine hover-chairs and beds on wheels. As Mary Oliver reminds us in her poem "Wild Geese," wherever we are, our inner and outer worlds are constantly offering themselves to our imaginations. We often simply do not see what is right in front of us. We look for and see what we expect, what has been seen there before. The things that are most familiar, the world of our daily lives, the emotions and physical sensations that quickly come and go, are hardly noticed or are labeled and judged in some habitual way that moves us past them with little or no real awareness. Our mind quickly labels what it perceives as good or bad, pleasant or unpleasant, useful or useless, and we move toward or away from what we see based on these often unconscious and automatic judgments.

Finding the stories we want to write, the play of light and shadow we want to photograph, the sounds we want to weave into songs in ways that are alive for ourselves and those to whom we will offer our work, requires learning to see, to be aware, to pay attention. Because our conditioned thinking is strongest in familiar settings, places where we think we know what we will see, it is often easier to be more awake in unfamiliar settings or situations. Without the authority of previous experience, we pay attention and see with fresh eyes both the new and the familiar. Years ago, returning one night from a trip to the Dominican Republic, I was suddenly aware of the number of electric lights glowing in the dark along the street and in the office buildings of Toronto's downtown skyline. Having recently been in a place with abandoned half-built buildings, intermittent electric power, and rough unpaved roads, I saw with new eyes the collective wealth and privilege of the country where I live. I became aware of what was normally too easy to ignore.

Sometimes it is small unfamiliar things that tweak my awareness and stimulate my imagination. Watching TV in my hotel room while on a book tour, I see a public service announcement that declares the local community's goal to make "Every Child a Success by Six!" And wonder, What would it look like to be a "success" by six? I see in my imagination the sad and serious image of a small boy in a suit and tie carrying a briefcase. How could anyone be a "failure" at six? Visiting the Book Expo in Los Angeles, I wander around the city and come across a sign for the Angels Flight Railway. Where are the angels fleeing to? What are they fleeing from and why? And why would angels need a railway? Couldn't they just fly away? Later, as I walk along the Pacific Ocean just steps from the park where groups of homeless men and women congregate, I pass a shop window displaying a beach towel priced at $390 and a small beaded case for carrying breath mints in your purse or pocket selling for $1000. And I wonder how a bath towel or a container for breath mints could be worth this kind of money to anyone.

The truth is that we do not need to go to new places to shake ourselves out of habitual ways of perceiving, to wake ourselves up to the world around us and let it stimulate our imagination. In fact, I suspect that if we keep searching for what is novel, relying on the unfamiliar to help us be aware, we will develop habitual ways of evaluating what is unfamiliar and then lose an immediate and direct experience of even the new. More important, most of our life is lived among the familiar, and seeking out novel situations and settings requires resources—time, energy, money, and opportunity—we may not have. We need to learn how to find the raw material for our creative work—images and stories, colors and sounds—wherever we are. We need to cultivate an attitude of open inquiry, of deep curiosity about what is happening within and around us, right now. This kind of inquiry does not seek answers as much as it raises the questions that jump-start the imagination. It is a vertical inquiry that requires going deeper instead of moving on too quickly to whatever is next.

All it takes is a willingness to pay attention, a desire to cultivate our sensory awareness, and a curiosity about the meaning our imagination can weave from the details of life. I lie in bed and notice I am feeling weary in a way that goes deeper than physical tiredness. I explore the feeling. Automatically, my mind labels it: I am discouraged. But, instead of thinking about why this feeling is there (something I am capable of doing for hours), I ask instead, What does it mean to be discouraged? What are the physical sensations that correspond to this feeling I call "discouraged"? I notice a heaviness, at first in my legs and arms, a lethargy, a feeling of never wanting to move again. I breathe into my body and focus on the feeling and discover that it collects to a point in my chest below the sternum. I consider: If this feeling had a color, a shape, a texture or taste, what would it be? I trace back through my day, my week, and see if I can discern when this feeling first arose. I clear my mind and focus on the feeling in my body, inviting an image that captures this feeling to come from the stillness. It may be a memory or an imagined picture. I open to finding a moment, a time or place or situation, that feels emblematic of this state I experience as "being discouraged." I think a little about the word, *dis-couraged,* being without courage, and I wonder what courage feels like, looks like, tastes like in contrast to the current reality I label "discouraged."

Being aware is being willing to stay with what is and follow it without expectation, holding an attitude of genuine curiosity and open inquiry. In the same way as I inquired into being discouraged, I often notice and question something I observe in the world around me: a scene before me at the local café, the interaction of friends at a gathering in my home, or the movement of weather across the landscape outside my living room window. Bringing a moment alive on the page is generally about finding a concrete way to convey the activity and feeling of that moment. And this requires specifics. To give specifics, we have to be aware of specifics. Having facilitated dozens of writing groups over the years, I can tell you without reservation that everyone and anyone can write well. By this I mean that anyone can produce writing that has a strong impact on the reader if they write about something that matters to them in a way that is specific. I am not suggesting that anyone or everyone can or should write a book. I have seen some folks struggle literally for months to come up with one sentence, one image that holds the power of what they want to communicate. Generally that struggle marks their journey from the general to the specific, as they become more and more aware of the taste, texture, feel, scent, color of something that matters to them.

Years ago, in a writing group I was facilitating, a woman who had recently been left by her husband wrote about her feelings of grief and abandonment. The group listened attentively as she read her pieces each week. We were not unsympathetic. Many of us had experienced the pain of betrayal and loss. But her descriptions failed to touch us, conveyed neither the inner or outer experience of being abandoned. She used familiar labels, telling us she was lonely, confused, in pain, suffering. Her writing talked *about* her experience but never took us into it. Over and over we listened, and each time I gently suggested that she sit with and explore her memories and feelings to discover just how they lived in her. What did abandonment look like, feel like, taste like? What was the color or the sound of betrayal? How did she know when she was feeling what we label "grief"? Then, one day, after weeks of writing what was at best an arm's-length report, she read us a short paragraph describing the day her husband left. I remember it vividly. It ended, *For what seemed like hours, the woman stood alone and unmoving at the kitchen window, watching the unlatched gate at the end of the sidewalk banging in the wind.*

I heard a small gasp from several people. A couple of others suddenly found their eyes filling with tears. We got it. There, in that one sentence, in the image of a woman standing immobilized and alone gazing out a window, in the sound of a thing neglected and blown in the wind, the writer took us to human despair and desolation—hers, ours, the world's.

The world offers itself to your imagination in every moment. And when we open to what is here, allowing it to stimulate our imagination, we create new worlds that invite others in. Sometimes we have to become aware of our expectations and learn to set them aside. Sometimes we have to bring to consciousness the hidden assumptions we have about ourselves and our place in the world. Robert Bly's poem "Things to Think" urges us to do both. With a light and yet penetrating touch, his words inspire me to learn to see, to think in new ways about the world.

THINGS TO THINK

Think in ways you've never thought before
If the phone rings, think of it as carrying a message
Larger than anything you've heard,
Vaster than a hundred lines of Yeats.

Think that someone may bring a bear to your door,
Maybe wounded and deranged; or think that a moose
Has risen out of the lake, and he's carrying on his antlers
A child of your own whom you've never seen.

When someone knocks on the door, think that he's about
To give you something large: tell you you're forgiven,
Or that it's not necessary to work all the time, or that it's
Been decided that if you lie down no one will die.
                                        Robert Bly

FOR CONTEMPLATION

- What if the material of great painting, inspired songs, or insightful stories is around and within you right now? What aspects of your experience or the sensory world around you do you dismiss as unworthy of being included in your creative work?

SEEING

- First, you have to decide if you *want* to see differently, to look beyond your habitual ways of perceiving yourself and the world. Consider what will happen if you give up being attached to having what you see agree with what you have seen before.

- Observe yourself without judgments as you walk through your day, lie in bed at night, sit in meditation. Notice how quickly and automatically your mind sorts and labels, dismissing some things and holding on to others, labeling thoughts, feelings, and sensations as pleasant or unpleasant, as what you like or dislike, as good or bad. Just be with this observation for a while.

- Consider slowing the process down just a little, waiting a moment in a neutral place before labeling what is in front of or within you. Consider what it means, feels like, tastes like to label what we are feeling or seeing in any way. Notice the effect of labeling, and of not labeling.

- Become aware of your own conditioned seeing by deliber-ately putting yourself in the company of those who, because they are from a different gender, age, class, religion, or eth-nic background, see things differently. Listen carefully and notice how you see things differently from others. Notice your response to the way others see things. Can you simply receive their perspective and let it affect you without label-ing it as good or bad, acceptable or unacceptable? Can you listen and watch without taking a position, even internally?

- Cultivate your curiosity. Carry a notebook and jot down things you notice. Write down questions about the things around you. Wonder. Why doesn't it snow as much when the temperature outside grows colder? (I recently asked this one and discovered in fact that the temperature drops because it is not snowing and rises when it is. My percep-tion had reversed the cause-effect relationship between temperature and precipitation.) Let your imagination play with the objects of your inquiry, using them metaphori-cally, wondering what would happen if they were suddenly different than they are.

- In your creative work, be specific. Look at your world and notice the details and weave those details into the work. While being specific, don't worry about being literal. Let the work be metaphoric where appropriate. Search for the emblematic moment that carries the fullness of what is being communicated. Sometimes one image or sound or phrase can hold the essence of a series of events or the complexity of emotions in one instance.

CREATING FROM DIFFERENT PERSPECTIVES

- In the shamanic teachings of the Medicine Wheel, everything can be viewed from the four directions of the circle.
  Doing creative work on a single theme from four different
  perspectives can make us aware of which perspective we
  usually take and which ones we generally ignore. Sometimes it helps in doing this exercise to sit or stand in the
  appropriate direction in the room where you are working. I
  have done this with writing, painting, and moving and can
  see no reason why it cannot be adapted to other forms of
  creative work (dance, composing, etc.). If you are working
  in forms like photography or filmmaking, which require a
  preliminary step of gathering material, you may write from
  each perspective in preparation for creating from each perspective.

- Pick a short story about something that happened to you
  in the past week. Sit for a moment and allow an incident to
  come to mind. Now write, paint, sing, or find the movement that reflects this incident strictly in terms of its physicality (where did it take place, what happened, who was
  there, what was said, heard, done, tasted, seen). Connect
  with specific sensory details of the incident as you create.
  Leave out the commentary, the judgments, the insights.
  Just describe or depict what happened. (West)

- Now, using the same story, do your creative work completely and solely in terms of emotion. What did each of
  the people involved feel? How did the feelings unfold?
  How were they expressed? (South)

- Again, using the same story, do your work from the place of understanding. What was the motivation of those involved, including you? What were the causes and the effects of what happened? What beliefs—yours or another's—were reflected in the choices or reactions that occurred? (North)

- And, for the final time, use the same story and express a sense of the meaning it has for you right now. If this incident had been a dream, what might your unconscious have been trying to tell you? Let your imagination go. What are the possible reasons for it coming to your mind and being your choice for this exercise? Imagine yourself telling the story to an elder, a wise old man or woman, and listening while this person tells you the meaning of this story for your life. What does this person say? (East)

WRITING EXERCISES

- Write, using sensory detail, about where you are right now. Don't worry about writing explanations or background for how you came to be here. Describe what is. Consider your frame of reference, the lens you use. Make it small—describe the fibers of your sleeve, the color and shape of a single blade of grass. Make it large—imagine how the spot you are in looks from the top of a tall building, an airplane, outer space.

- Imagine that you had to lose, had to wipe out completely, a year you have already lived. Which year would you choose? Describe the main events of that year and why you chose it. Consider the impact losing this year might have. If all events are effects of former causes, consider what would not have happened in your life if the events of that year, the ones you are willing to let go, had never happened.

- Describe an emblematic moment, a vivid sensory detail or one small story that holds within it one of the following:

   —a sense of who you were as a child

   —a sense of your family

   —a sense of a community in which you have lived

   —a moment when you realized that you were no longer a child

   —a moment when you realized that adults were not perfect, were flawed human beings who are often as confused as children

   —your sense of trust or distrust in the world and life itself

   —a moment that illustrates the character of someone you love

- There is a game I played as a child that I now use as a writing warm-up. From the time I was nine years old I would stand somewhere alone, with my eyes closed, and turn around, stopping when I had lost all sense of direction. Then I would open my eyes and focus at random on something in front of me. It could be anything: a leaf, a blade of grass, a piece of stray garbage, a lamp, the floral pattern in my curtains, the spine of a book next to my bed. And the task I set for myself, the game I played, was to make up a story that would use whatever my eyes had settled upon when they first opened to articulate some lesson about living. I would open my eyes and focus on whatever came into view and begin writing, "A pine cone can teach us about life . . ." letting my imagination run to something like ". . . to fulfill its purpose, to release its seeds so that new trees can grow, it has to open, to unfold. . . ." I'm not claiming that I received any particularly startling insights about life by doing this. But it was never about the content, about achieving results. It was about finding connections and feeling the thrill of stretching my imagination to create meaning out of whatever was in front of me. Thinking of it now I am surprised by the unspoken certainty I had as a child that all things contain the wholeness of life and are available to our imagination's ability to create and touch the meaning at the core of life. Try it. Stand in a place, outdoors or in, and close your eyes. Twirl slowly on the spot until you have lost a sense of the direction you are facing. Stop and open your eyes, allowing them to focus on one specific point in front of you. Whatever is in this line of vision, use it to begin writing about some aspect of life. Begin with the phrase,

Life is like . . .

naming the object you first saw when opening your eyes and continuing to expand upon the metaphor.

five

DOING THE WORK

Occasionally during an interview someone will ask me, "What advice do you have for young writers?"

My response is always the same. Regardless of the age or experience of the writer, the best advice I can give about learning how to write, about improving both the quality and quantity of your writing, is simply to write. Write every day if you can. Write when you are upset or suffering, and write when you are elated and happy. Write about what is in front of you, what you remember, and what you imagine as possible. Write with pen or pencil or by computer, early in the morning or late at night or on your lunch break. Write about what you know and about what you do not know. Write about what you want to write about, and write about what you do not want to write about.

We learn how to create by creating. Reading inspiring writing, going to art galleries, getting helpful tips from experienced writers or artists, taking a course, joining a group, going on regular retreats, getting feedback, setting deadlines, creating a supportive environment—all of these help to develop your ability to do your creative work to the extent that they increase the amount of creative work you do. If you want to learn how to write, paint, compose, sculpt, or dance, you must write, paint, compose, sculpt, dance. Everything in this book—all the insights, exercises, suggestions, and stories—are aimed at one outcome: to encourage you to do your creative work more. It is my experience that those who engage in the creative process by actually doing the work are those who learn how.

We live in a culture that values speed. For many, anything that can't be learned over the course of a weekend workshop is simply not worth the effort. The result is a plethora of workshops that promise the impossible, claiming that you can learn how to write a best-selling novel or find your soul mate or eradicate all fear from your life forever in only two days. Maybe we can't be blamed for hoping that instant gratification is possible. Most of us are so busy running between the demands of our jobs and our responsibilities at home that finding time to engage in learning that takes more than forty-eight hours often feels out of our reach.

When I was a child I wanted to be an artist, a painter. My parents bought me an easel, oil paints, and Masonite boards, and I began. The results were not encouraging. No matter how carefully I studied the pictures and step-by-step instructions in the art books I pored over at the local bookstore, my trees still looked like turquoise balloons and my people looked like they were made out of bright pink Silly Putty. Other than the occasional Saturday morning art class at the local Kiwanis Club, no art courses were offered in the small northern Ontario community where I grew up. I kept at it for a few years but gave up my fantasy of going to art college when my painting did not improve appreciably. A few years later, while studying sociology at university, I remember telling a young man I'd just met in the pub that I had wanted to be an artist but had lacked the talent so had not pursued it.

"Bullshit!" he replied abruptly. I was offended. How could he know if I had talent or not? I pointed out somewhat tersely that he had just met me, had never seen any of my paintings.

Smelling of beer and stale cigarettes, he leaned in closer to me and spoke with surprising conviction. "I don't need to know you or see your work to know that you quit without even knowing if you had talent or not. What are you, nineteen?" I conceded I was, thinking that he could be no more than twenty-two himself. "Then you never gave it a chance. You haven't put enough into it to know if you have any talent or not. It takes time, time and work, to discover what you can do, what you might do creatively. You gave up before you even began, before you had a chance to find out if you had any talent or not!"

I can't say that he convinced me. I still felt I was lacking some basic talent for painting. And maybe I was. But the talent I was lacking may not have been an innate ability to mix colors or see shapes, conceive images or wield a palette knife. The talent I was lacking may have been perseverance, the willingness to do something badly over and over again until I began to learn how to do it well, began to find my way of making what was on the canvas reflect what was in my head and heart.

I may not have been convinced, but I never forgot the certainty in that young man's face and the twinge I felt within myself as I wondered if he might be right. I'd always prided myself on being a hard worker, a diligent student, a responsible employee. No one had ever accused me of giving up on something. I did not think of myself as a quitter. But the truth was that I was reluctant to do things I could not do well quickly. I did not like failing. I was very attached to doing well fast.

Some years later I heard musician and composer John Cougar Mellencamp being interviewed on the radio, and I was reminded of that young man from the pub. Mellencamp said that people generally fail in creative endeavors because they assume that great artists produce great works of art from the moment they begin. He postulated that for every masterpiece Renoir produced he had painted dozens if not hundreds of paintings that were just not very good. As a composer, Mellencamp had realized that he had to be willing to compose literally thousands of bad songs, songs that were hardly worth singing and certainly not worth recording, if he wanted to write one great song. Mellencamp pointed out that when an artist puts his or her work out into the world it appears to emerge fully formed. Those who receive the completed work, the piece deemed worthy of sharing, have no idea how long a process was involved, how many previous incarnations hit the trash can or were painted or recorded over.

Slowly it began to sink in: I had to be willing to keep at it, to learn from the doing. If I wanted to learn how to write or paint or do any form of creative work, I had to be willing to do it over and over again, even if the results were not what I wanted.

I once heard Robert Bly talking about poet William Stafford. Stafford apparently made it a practice, a commitment, to write one poem a day. Once, when an interviewer asked him what he did when the poem he produced was no good, Stafford replied, "I lower my standards."

This same advice was given to me more than ten years ago by Gifford Booth, one of the instructors and founding directors of

TAI Resources in New York City. Attending a weekend workshop on expanding creative expression, trying to find my own way of performing poetry I love, I was horrified when Gifford advised me to lower my standards. For a perfectionist this is tough but necessary advice. Nothing stops the creative flow and obstructs the only path to learning to create—repeated trial and error—like being wedded to doing it perfectly, trying to get it right the first or second or even tenth or twentieth time. And nothing frees up the flow, opens the door to the learning that can come only with repeated experience, like lowering your standards, giving yourself permission to write the worst possible drivel that has ever hit the page.

In their book *Art and Fear,* authors David Bayles and Ted Orland tell a story that illustrates how lowered expectations encourage the repetition necessary for creative skill development. A ceramics teacher divided a class of novice students into two groups. One group was told that their final mark would be based completely on the number of the pots they produced. More pots, higher grade. The other group was told that they would be graded purely on their ability to produce one perfect pot. The perhaps not-so-surprising outcome was that the best-quality pots were all produced by those who made the largest quantity of pots—those who, without attachment to result, had set out to make as many pots as possible. They had learned how to make better and better pots. It seems that even when we are not deliberately trying to do so, we inevitably learn from our mistakes.

Perseverance is proportional to commitment. It is possible that aside from my impatience and desire to do well quickly, the thing that kept me from pursuing my development as a painter was simply a lack of commitment, a lack of desire. It didn't matter enough to me. Or perhaps I had not yet realized how much it did matter. In Pat Schneider's book *The Writer as an Artist,* she advises that if you are trying to write and finding it painfully hard and know you can quit, go ahead and quit. She also advises that if you find you cannot quit, you might as well surrender to simply doing it, to writing even if the process is difficult and the outcome dubious. I could quit painting, so I did. But writing was different for me. Although I similarly feared I lacked potential as a writer, I felt compelled to keep writing. Perhaps it was easier to fail repeatedly within the protected privacy of my journals instead of on a canvas everyone passing by could see. For years I rarely showed anyone my writing, and I did not feel that writing for a living was a practical aspiration. In fact, it never really occurred to me that this was a possibility. But I continued to fill journal after journal with musings, stories, poems, and diatribes. Gradually my writing began to take on a certain flavor, a particular voice expressing reoccurring images and themes.

Repetition in our creative work does not simply teach skill development. It takes the process deeper, revealing truths that we simply do not notice when we move on too quickly. Years ago I attended a workshop called an "Enlightenment Intensive." The basic format of the workshop was the repetition of one question for three days. People rotated through different partners and were asked the same question over and over again, literally hundreds of times over the course of the retreat. All other distractions— chatting between sessions or over meals, reading or writing, going for a walk—were put aside, eradicated by the strict schedule and clear guidelines.

My question, the question most people are given on their first retreat, was, *Who am I?* Over and over again the man or woman opposite me said, "Tell me who you are." My job was to receive the inquiry, become aware of my direct internal response to it, and communicate my experience to my partner. My partner could only acknowledge receiving my reply with a simple "Thank you" or ask for more information with the words "Clarify please" or "Again."

I started out curious to see what would happen. As a student and teacher of spiritual practices for many years, I began by giving what I thought were pretty insightful, lucid, erudite answers. Then I moved through a vast range of responses: boredom, annoyance and irritation, a certain blank numbness, mental meandering, the desire to entertain, trying to reach for profound insight (usually followed immediately by increased boredom and irritation). Finally I simply had to give up wanting to look or sound like anything in particular. Eventually I just didn't care anymore whether or not I was sounding profound or stupid, attentive or bored, polite or rude. All the ideas I have about who I am, all the stories I tell myself, had been told, and they all rang pretty hollow. I didn't care what the other person thought anymore or whether or not I even reached a profound truth about who I was. Repetition had done the impossible—it had lowered my standards. And still the request was made and I replied. And then, out of the absence of expectation that repetition had created, something else began to happen—a new freedom, a real and deeper willingness to start each time from the place of not knowing who I was, of being genuinely curious, of wondering right along with the questioner, *Who is this being sitting here?* And with that willingness, with the dropping away of the hope or desire to get it right, I caught a glimpse of something new; I sank into a direct if brief experience of who—or perhaps more accurately what—I am. It took my breath away. It moved through my body like fire and left my partner and me laughing with the sheer delight of being.

Repetition in the creative process can bring us to this sense of open-ended inquiry, to the freedom to experience ourselves and the world directly. I am not suggesting here that what is repeated is always profound, but the willingness to do our creative work repeatedly, even when the same themes or images or stories appear, opens us to honing our skills and also to the possibility of seeing what our ideas about reality—inner or outer—cause us to miss. When I was younger and reread my journals I would become discouraged by how many themes and stories and images were repeated. My angst over not being loved the way I thought I wanted to be loved by the man in my life was there in stark and sometimes not very inspiring prose or poetry. And there it was again, months or years later, the same anguish, a similar story, perhaps with a different partner, perhaps with the same one. And I despaired at how often my writing, whether fiction or fact, pointed to and reflected a hopeless drivenness, a sense of failing to live some elusive life's purpose. "Oh, for heaven's sake, Oriah, it's the same thing over and over. Give it up!" I moaned as I read.

Then I went to a screening of a film about a painter, Philip Guston, who had been a compatriot of Jackson Pollock. His daughter, Musa Meyer, spoke at the screening. The thing that fascinated me most was seeing the repetition of images in the paintings he had done over the years. Over and over again, across decades, throughout different styles and evolving techniques, there were reoccurring images of hooded figures resembling members of the Klu Klux Klan in full ritual garb. The white triangles and dark eyeholes of their headgear appeared again and again, popping up amid abstract swirls of color or clearly depicted in realistic scenes. Musa said that there had been extensive speculation among art critics of the time about what this image was meant to convey or what place it held in her father's psyche. Certainly he painted in a time when the struggle for human rights made the Klan a prominent player in the national news. But her father never had any clear explanation for it, never claimed to completely understand what this image was meant to convey in his paintings. He just kept painting, and the image kept reappearing, not in every painting but consistently throughout his work.

What impressed me most about this story was Guston's willingness to allow the creative process to have its way with him, his willingness to repeatedly paint the same image over and over if that's what came. Of course, no two images were ever identical, but the theme was there and he was willing to let it repeat within his work, even though (or perhaps because) he did not understand why it was there or exactly what it was meant to communicate to him or others. Perhaps it was this honoring of the value of repetition that allowed him to be unattached to outcome. At one point the filmmaker stays with Guston, filming him throughout several days and nights of rigorous painting. We watch as he pours his life's energy into a huge canvas for hours at a time, and then, when it is done, he stands back and looks at the canvas for a few moments, a burning cigarette dangling from his hand. Smiling and shaking his head, he shrugs and grabs a wide brush and, dipping it into a bucket of white paint, paints over the entire canvas, obliterating the work of days. And he begins again.

Something shifted in me when I watched that film. It was a little like waking up. I'd heard about the necessity in creative work to be willing to make mistakes, willing to do the work over and over, willing to let go of attachment to results. But I had never seen it so explicitly in action. I remember thinking, "Oh, so that's how you do it. You just keep starting again."

At some point, of course, you may decide that the work—the poem, the painting, the song or performance—is complete and ready to be shared with others. Most of the writing I do is not worth publishing or even sharing with another individual. In chapter 11, I will talk about knowing when something is complete and about sharing it with others, but for now I simply want to assert that a necessary prerequisite for engaging in the creative process fully is the willingness to do it again and again.

All this focus on the need for repetition may make it sound like creative work is a tedious task requiring great amounts of willpower and energy. If I think of writing as something I have to do over and over for years, something I have to find endless energy for, I begin to feel too tired to pick up a pen. If I think of it as my job as a writer to write or decide that I must write to improve my writing, it becomes less and less of a joy. And I write first and foremost because the process brings me joy. If it ceased to bring me joy I would stop.

So, although I know repetition is necessary both to develop skills and to open to the deepest insights and most nourishing images and stories that I can co-create, I am careful how I label this process for myself so as not to make it one more thing on a long list of things I have to do. Although I have called myself a writer and have sometimes found it a useful label for allowing me to claim the time and space needed to write, I know it is only a label and not the truth. Years ago I had a dream. In it, an old man I have seen in my dreams for many years smiled and said to me,

"Do not confuse what you do with who you are, Oriah. You are not a writer, although you may at times write. You are life unfolding in human form, an awareness within which writing, along with many other things—eating, sleeping, making love, walking in the sun, feeling sad or glad—arises. There is no writer, only writing."

There is no writer, only writing; no painter, only painting; no composer, only composing. . . . This idea frees us from the sometimes oppressive notion that we make the creative work happen. The human neurological system and awareness is but one of the places where creative work arises and through which it happens. Thinking of it this way, we can let the creative work be whatever it is. We can arrive at our desks or studios, our journals or easels or keyboards or cameras, excited to see what might happen and content to let it be what it is, to repeat the process over and over. This perspective can keep us from viewing creative work as a means to an end, as something with a hoped-for outcome, and help us see it rather as an end in itself.

It's not easy to hang on to the idea of creative work as an end in itself. And I am not suggesting that any form of creative work that is successfully marketed in the world, bringing its author limited or expansive fame and fortune, is not really creative work. But I am suggesting that the necessary willingness to bring your self to the process over and over again is severely diminished if the goal is to create a product that will be a means to other ends. I am discouraged by the number of people I meet who want to learn how to write in order to promote themselves or achieve some legitimacy for their career as a management consultant or public speaker. One public speaker and facilitator told me, "You just can't succeed unless you have a book!" Somewhere along the line we have accepted the notion that if you knew what you were doing in just about any field, you would have written a book about it. But writing and speaking or consulting involve different processes, require and develop different skills. It's not that public speakers or consultants should not or cannot write or paint or compose or dance. Many people have multiple skills and interests they can bring to common themes. But the deepest creative impulse does not serve other ends, cannot be found and followed and developed as a means to an end.

Leaving my doctor's office a little over a year ago, I crossed paths with a woman I had met briefly at a social gathering months before. A bright, articulate, attractive middle-aged woman who has had a career as a television anchorwoman, Andrea knows I have written for years. She greeted me warmly.

"Oriah, how wonderful to bump into you here. Just last night a group of friends and I were talking about how much we all want to be writers." Having facilitated writing groups for many years, I found my mind immediately sifting through helpful suggestions for how to start writing. Before I could respond, Andrea continued, "But we realized that none of us actually wants to write!"

I had nothing to say to that.

What does it mean to say you want to be a writer but you don't want to write, want to be an artist but you don't want to paint or sculpt, want to be a composer but you don't want to compose? I suspect it means you want to live the life you imagine writers or painters or sculptors or composers live, and I suspect that the life you imagine does not focus on the need to consistently and repeatedly take yourself to your computer or canvas or keyboard and do the work. I suspect those who want to be writers but don't want to write are imagining themselves going on all-expense-paid international book tours, staying at five-star hotels, ordering room service, and raiding the minibar. The fantasy probably includes images of being interviewed on television and radio and for the *New York Times* and having every word you utter carefully listened to as if all these years of living really had made you wonderfully wise and startlingly insightful. It probably means you want to be invited to speak at large conferences or sought after to do readings at gatherings of thoughtful, intelligent people. It may mean you imagine that all writers drink copious amounts of Scotch and get away with behaving badly into the wee hours of the morning. Or maybe you imagine that most writers are whiling away their hours in the peace of pristine mountain retreats, scribbling bits of wisdom that effortlessly come to them whole and complete and sending them off to an eager publisher who has paid large sums in advance for these gems.

Of course some writers do receive handsome advances, some drink Scotch, and more than a few—like everyone else—on occasion behave badly. And if someone engaged in creative work is lucky enough to have his or her work shared in a commercially successful way, they may even be interviewed and sought after— for a while. It's not really surprising that people have a distorted view of what it means to live a life of doing creative work. Like the actual process, which may result in a finished book or painting or song, the life of someone engaged in creative work is largely invisible. The visible portion, the tip of the proverbial iceberg, is the book tour, the gallery opening, the press piece about a small sliver of the lives of a very few artists. And even though we all know we are not getting a complete picture from these snippets, it is tempting to be seduced by glimpses of a life we imagine to be much more glamorous and gratifying or idyllic and inspiring than the daily logistics of carpools, utility bills, and cleaning up after the dog.

But the bottom line is that writers write, painters paint, composers compose, photographers photograph, and dancers dance. Over and over again. Sometimes we use the same stories and images, sounds and movements. Sometimes we work on the same themes using different stories and images, sounds and movements. Sometimes we create the unexpected and never repeated. Sometimes we create between interviews and publicity tours. More often we create between dental appointments and taking our children to hockey practice. But we do our creative work. It's how we learn *how* to do the creative work. And sometimes we become tired and discouraged. Sometimes we do not want to see the same image emerge on the canvas, find the same theme surface in the story we are writing. Sometimes we are afraid we will never be able to write or paint or compose or dance or film the wholeness or beauty or truth we ache to produce. And in these moments we take ourselves out into the world and let our sexuality, our love of the sensual beauty of this physical life, and our spirituality, our experience of the truth we ache for, find us and rekindle our passion to create. We let the dance between the world and our imaginations move us. And we begin again, painting or writing or composing, moving or photographing or filming. It's how we dip down into that well of creative potential and weave a story or create an image or find just a single phrase of melody that takes the breath away. It's how we pray, how we participate in life. Over and over again.

FOR CONTEMPLATION

- What if perseverance is proportional to commitment? In what ways do you find it difficult to persevere? Is there a lack of commitment? Could you quit?

LEARNING TO DO CREATIVE WORK

- Complete the following phrases repeatedly:

    Today I am willing to do _____ *badly.*
    Today I will lower my standards in how I . . .
    I do _____ *badly, but I do it because . . .*

- Complete the following phrases:

    I am committed to . . .
    I find it difficult to persevere at . . .
    I am patient with . . .
    I am impatient with . . .

- Substitute the phrase *I am patient with . . .* with the phrase *I trust . . .* Do both phrases ring true? Can you write more about this?

- Substitute the phrase *I am impatient with . . .* with the phrase *I do not trust . . .* Do both phrases ring true? Can you write more about this?

- Make a list of all the roles you fulfill and with which you identify—mother, father, writer, artist, secretary, teacher, student. . . . Be specific. Now, fill in the blanks:

*I am not a _____ (mother, writer, teacher . . .) but
the place where _____ (mothering, writing, teaching
. . .) arises.*

Notice, without judgment, your reactions.

WRITING EXERCISE

- Each day answer the following questions for three to five
  minutes each. Commit to doing this every day for a set period of time (a week minimum, a month maximum). Let
  your answers go wherever the writing takes you. Be as concrete as you can. How would what you are writing about
  feel, taste, smell? What would it look like? Bring the answers to life with specific details. Let emblematic images
  take the place of and flesh out abstract ideas. Is there a
  story, an image, a sound or scent from your life that illustrates an answer to the question better than writing what
  you think about the question? Each time you write an answer, ask yourself, What is the truest thing I can say in response to this question in this moment?

  Who are you? I am . . .

  Where did you come from? I came from . . .

  Where are you going? I am going . . .

  Why are you here? I am here . . .

At the end of the week or month you have set aside to repeatedly do this exercise, reread all of your answers. What do you notice? Are there any surprises? How did your answer change with

the repetition of the question? Are there reoccurring themes, images, or ideas? If so, choose one and commit to staying with it for a set period of time, to write about it for ten minutes a day for a week or a month. How does it change, grow, or lose or gain energy or interest for you?

six

DEVELOPING A
CREATIVE PRACTICE

A couple of years ago I heard Tom Robbins, author of many novels including *Still Life with Woodpecker* and *Even Cowgirls Get the Blues,* speak at a conference. After his talk someone in the audience asked him what he does when the muse, that guardian and carrier of the elusive spark of inspiration, does not come to him when he sits down to write. Tom responded without hesitation that whether or not the muse visits is none of his business. His business, he said, is to show up at his writing desk at his usual time each day. If the muse arrives and he writes inspired prose, wonderful. If not, well, he has done his bit by showing up fully.

The bottom line is that no matter how much we prime the creative pump, how willing we are to repeatedly begin and continue our creative work, how open we are to expanding our ways of seeing, we cannot guarantee that we will be able to find and ride the sought-after wave of inspiration when we want it. We can't make it happen, but we can increase the odds considerably by doing our part, by showing up. This sounds easy enough, but since most of us do not live in an isolated cork-lined room where unobtrusive helpers leave meals at our door and carry away the dirty dishes, since most of us have to take care of ourselves, our homes, and often other people, a hundred legitimate reasons for not showing up present themselves daily. Of course, if you are terribly disciplined you will walk right past all of the other things that call for your attention and simply do your creative work. However, relying on your willpower to get you there takes resolve and energy, which are not always easily accessible. The alternative, and the easiest way to ensure that you will show up to do your creative work even when the unexpected happens, is to treat that work as a practice. A practice is something you consciously do on a regular basis by following a particular routine or structure that allows you to do it even when other things beckon or you simply don't feel like doing it.

Every author I have ever met follows some kind of routine while working on a specific project, and of course no two routines are exactly the same. I have a practice that ensures that I write daily even when I am not working on a particular book but am simply writing in my journal. Such a practice helps keep my creative muscles limber and stops me from making the process of writing into simply a means to the end of producing a book. Once again you have to experiment, see what works for you, and be ruthlessly honest with yourself by using only one criterion: Do I do more or less creative work when I follow this routine, engage in this practice? Remember the ceramics class mentioned in the previous chapter. If you do more creative work, you will eventually do better creative work.

A structured way of starting your creative work enables you, on the days when you really do not feel like doing the work, to stay present and keep moving one incremental step at a time into the process. Treating your creative work as a practice that fully engages you for its own sake enables you to more easily let go of fears about impending deadlines or worries that no one will ever be waiting or willing to receive what you are creating. When you are writing, you are simply writing. When you are painting, you are simply painting. A practice helps you to bring your full attention to the present, to the sentence you are writing, the movement you are making, the image you are creating right now.

Setting up a practice begins with finding a place for that practice. Often this is dictated by circumstances. There simply may be no separate room in your home to claim as space for your creative work. I urge you to carefully weigh the great benefit gained by having such a room against the debatable need for both a living room and a family room, an eat-in kitchen and a dining room, or a separate laundry room or wine cellar, if you happen to be lucky enough to have any of these. Considerations about use of space may be literally debatable if you live with others, but having this conversation can be your opportunity to convey to those who love you just how important it is to you to do your creative work and carve out the space that is needed to help this happen. Claiming the space in a collective living situation may be the first step in claiming your right and honoring your need to do creative work.

For years, when my children were away at school in the daytime and in bed early in the evening, my desk sat in the corner of our living room, the only available spot in our small home. If the time you have available for doing creative work is time when other people are in your home and awake, the only rule about where you do the work is that the room, even if it is used for other purposes at other times, must have a door, and everyone must understand that a closed door is not to be knocked upon or opened unless something important is on fire. Of course, different forms of creative expression require different kinds of space. I can write in places where few could dance or sculpt or paint. Some forms may require a space that is outside the home. But the chances of doing your creative work regularly as a practice, if only in a preliminary form, are greatly increased if the space where you do it is easily accessible.

I have moved my desk to different locations throughout the homes I have lived in over the years. In my current home, where I have lived for just over a year, I have put my writing desk, at different times, in the room above the garage, in my bedroom, and in the living room, where I am presently working. I have even spent some time writing at the kitchen table. The current choice is made possible because my sons are grown and no longer living with me and my husband works elsewhere all day. It is preferable because of a very efficient woodstove in the living room and subzero temperatures outside. It has occurred to me that while some people make a new home their own by setting up altars or making love in all the different rooms of the house, I am in a similar if somewhat unconscious process of claiming this space by writing in different locations throughout my home. But then, I think of creative work as one way of making love to the world and the places where we do this work as altars—sensual, physical representations of the sacred, where we hope to call in and focus all available energies of both seen and unseen worlds. Not even this aspect of the creative process—finding a place to do the work—is separable from our sexuality and our spirituality.

Of course, like everything else, we can use the task of setting up a space for our creative work as a way to avoid the work itself. My dear friend Kris spent many months setting up a space in her home for painting. She created a stunningly beautiful studio in a sunroom with hardwood floors, vivid multicolored silk blinds on the windows, and an elegant lounger set in the corner. The space was a piece of art itself, and Kris, after all those months of industrious work, never did any of the painting she had anticipated doing there. But she did wisely enroll in a course in interior design. Sometimes you have to give up the idea of the creative work you thought you were going to do in order to let the creative work you ache to do happen.

I have discovered only one consistent rule about location: I need to write in a spot that is different from the place where I do business, the place where I pay bills, return phone calls, answer e-mails, do the financial books, and design workshops. When I wrote in the room above the garage, which also serves as my business office, this meant putting my writing desk as far away as possible from my business desk, telephone, and filing cabinets. Luckily, it is a large room. The state of mind and heart I need to take care of the minutiae of business-related details is very different from the internal state I experience when I am in the flow of writing, and the former can too easily sidetrack the latter if I put myself in proximity to the siren song of logistical details. Recently I heard a friend who is a talented composer and musician express her frustration at the way in which teaching music lessons, arranging performances, and marketing recordings eats up all the time she wants to dedicate to composing. I suggested she try a similar separation of the spaces dedicated to business and creativity. Despite the fact that she has a beautiful and spacious studio where she meets students, clients, and business partners, she created a space exclusively for composing in a tiny utility shed behind her home. She has found that providing herself this space has increased the time and energy she has to devote to the task that lies at the heart of all she does—composing music.

Again, this is very individual. Some folks may be able to sit down at a desk piled high with unpaid bills, telephone messages, and contracts that need reviewing and focus on their creative work. But we don't get any extra points for, and we don't produce better work by, doing it in the hardest possible way. If the goal is to go more deeply and more frequently into our creative work, we need to set it up in a way that gives us the best possible chance of having this happen. Years ago I remember reading a quote that the chaos in artists' lives should reside in their work, in the sometimes erratic and unpredictable process of creating, and not in the space where they are working. Of course, one person's chaos is another person's interior design, and if you are someone who simply does not even notice clutter, you may not be distracted by it. But if you are finding yourself having a hard time consistently getting to the work you long to do, it may be useful to ask yourself if this work could be done with greater ease if you cleaned up or organized some of the flotsam and jetsam of life—the stray socks, unfolded laundry, and unsigned school reports—that may be strewn throughout the space you want to use. And if you find this kind of thing daunting, start surveying your friends and family to see who is particularly good at organizing the stuff of life and would be willing to help you get your space organized.

Aside from finding space where I am not distracted from my creative work, I use three important components of daily practice to go into writing: a time of prayer and contemplation, which allows me to slow down and clarify my intent; a time of physical movement, usually yoga and a walk, which grounds me in the physicality of my own body and the material world I want to draw from to bring my writing alive; and a time of writing in my journal.

I am not suggesting that everyone needs to pray before they begin their creative work, although I do think it would be helpful for everyone to find something that serves the purpose that prayer has in my life. This means finding a way to connect with your spirituality, your direct experience of the essential presence within and around you, your ability to be fully here now. For me prayer is a way to stop, to slow down and bring to my consciousness the infinite array of creation, the powers of the seen and unseen worlds. I do not think that God, the Sacred Mystery, the Great Mother, the divine life force—whatever you want to call the source of all that is around and within us—leaves or forsakes us if we do not pray. It is always there, but my attention is often elsewhere. Praying is a way of reminding myself of the depth and breadth of the Mystery in which I am held, in which I participate every day. I use a set of twenty-two prayers I was taught many years ago by the shaman with whom I apprenticed and the group of old women I often see in my night dreams. These prayers, based on an intertribal shamanic tradition, are prescribed enough that I can do them even when I do not feel like praying, when the words do not flow spontaneously because I am tired or discouraged or distracted. But they are also open-ended enough that I can add to them and express my heart's desire when I am moved to do so. I pray to remember the fertile emptiness that is within the form I am, the void from which those quantum particles of which all things are made continuously appear and disappear. I pray to feel over and over my interconnectedness with all of life. I pray to bring my attention to the world inside and around me. I offer thanks for the opportunity to write. I ask for guidance that the words I write might serve to alleviate suffering in the world.

This latter piece, the prayer of supplication and dedication, is a declaration of intent. Over and over it requires that I be clear about why I do this, why I write. Whether or not you are comfortable with the idea of prayer—and I understand why it may be a foreign or downright alienating concept to many—it is useful to begin your creative work with a few moments of quiet contemplation and to state for yourself your intent for the work you will do today. To what do you dedicate your creative efforts? What purpose do you want your work to serve? Sometimes my intent is very specific—to finish chapter 6 today. But always I place what I do within the general intent of being fully present with the work and dedicating what I do to serving that which is larger than me, that which I experience as a loving presence. By this I do not mean that I am simply hoping that the words I write will offer some comfort or consolation or inspiration to future readers, although I do always pray that the words I write do no harm and may offer to any who read them what they need for their greatest good. Often I am writing something that will never be shared, and yet I still pray that the creative work I do might contribute to the world. I see this as possible primarily because the very space we hold, the way we are with ourselves and each other, ripples out into the world. If our creative work helps us to be with what is in this moment with a compassionate heart and willing acceptance of what we cannot control, if it enables us to open to the joy of being alive, to seeing and co-creating meaning that sustains us, these are the things that will ripple out into the world from us whether or not anyone ever reads the words or music we have written or sees the painting or play or film we have created. And just as the flutter of the butterfly's wings may contribute to creating a hurricane, so what ripples out from us may have undreamed-of effects on the world.

I don't mean to imply that we must be trying to save the world with our creative work. We will probably produce better work if we hold significantly lower expectations. Maybe we just want to make people smile or find a new and lighter perspective on our tendency to get tied up in the knots of our inner dramas. Maybe we just want to entertain ourselves or others with a good story. Yet how would any of these not ease, if only a little, the suffering in the world? The purpose of dedicating your work to some purpose just a little larger than personal gratification or paying the bills is to recognize that we are interconnected and so what we do and how we do it affect the whole, consciously or unconsciously. Declaring intent is an effort to create consciously, to recognize that our creative work is not separable from the spiritual or sexual existence we share as human beings.

One decision that has to be made when developing a practice of creative work is how often and when we will do the practice. For a practice to be supportive it needs to be done on a regular basis, preferably daily. While some forms of creative expression, like writing, are easy to do in short, daily time periods, others require modification to find a form that fits the time available. A painter whose work necessitates setup and cleanup time may find that a practice of daily sketching enables him or her to productively use weekly or monthly sessions set aside for painting.

I confess that I am a morning person. I begin moving into my practice as soon as I wake up. On the rare occasion when I have left it to later in the day, I have regretted doing so. There is an old saying: as we begin, so shall we continue. Something is lost when we do not begin our day consciously. Even if you do not have an opportunity or inclination to do your creative work until later in the day, I highly recommend taking some time for contemplation, however brief, when you first rise. At the start of the day a stillness, an attitude of openness, is available before you are completely awake and going at full throttle. If you will be doing creative work later in the day, a second brief moment of stillness when that time arrives can reconnect you to the intent you set and the freshness you found, if only for a moment, upon first rising.

When I crawl out of bed in the morning, I get a cup of hot water and lemon and go to my altar. I light a candle and burn some dried herbs in an abalone shell, moving the smoke over and around my body. One of the things we know about rituals is that they carve a pathway into a particular state of mind and body. If they are meaningful to those who do them, ritual actions can create a sacred container, a space that is set apart from the everyday chores and logistical concerns that sometimes threaten to consume us.

We are sexual—physical, sensual—beings whose state of mind and heart is often triggered by what our senses perceive. One of the strongest triggers for the human mind that will conjure remembered times and states of consciousness is scent. Ceremonial smudge is a mixture of dried herbs—cedar, sage, sweetgrass, and lavender—used by many traditional tribal peoples to both cleanse themselves and their ceremonial space and to signal to unseen forces that they are about to send out a voice, to open themselves to being conscious of what is within and around them. I have used this way of beginning ceremonial time for almost twenty years, so the scent of the smoke that rises and curls around me as I burn the herbs is a powerful indicator to my conscious and unconscious mind that I am crossing a threshold, leaving smaller concerns aside for the moment to focus on what matters. It is also a signal to those living with me that I am temporarily unavailable, that I am engaged in writing or prayer or other inner work. You could use any fragrance that has meaning to you with a scented candle or aromatic oil as a way of reinforcing your movement into a time of creative practice. I know one author who sharpens five or six pencils just before he begins to write each day, confessing that it is the scent of freshly shaved wood and lead that signals to him that the writing is about to begin.

Clearly my spiritual training and practices are interwoven with how I approach my creative work, but no elaborate background in any spiritual tradition is needed. All you need to do is develop a set of practices that can take you into your creative work, practices that have enough structure to help you do the work whether you feel like it or not. One of the ways to do this is to let time be your container by setting a specific project length or time frame within which to work. Some people decide they will work each day until they have filled a set number of pages with writing, taken a certain number of photos, written a certain number of bars of music. Others decide they will work for a specific time period. Either way, the internal agreement provides a container that ensures that you will keep working, that lets you sidestep the continual inner debate about whether or not you should continue or stop. This can be helpful when things are not coming easily, when it would be easy to stop and the only thing that keeps you going and makes you available to the flow that may or may not happen is the established routine of filling five pages or working for a set time.

When I am writing the first draft of a book I generally write four or five days a week for seven hours a day with three brief breaks during the day for food and tea. But whether or not I am writing a book, I always write in my journal in the morning during or after my contemplative prayers. Often the prayers themselves open some new way of seeing, spark some reflection on my day or the world that I feel compelled to write down. Many years ago, when I began to do the prayers, I felt I should complete the full set before I began to write, but I have learned to trust the impulse to write when it comes and to follow it by writing until it is spent and then to return to the prayers once again.

If nothing is immediately present and itching to be written, I often revisit favorite warm-ups such as *What would you do if you knew you had one year (or six months) to live?* or *What would you do if you knew you couldn't fail?* Generally, I set a time limit of twenty minutes on the practice of structured journaling, although this is a minimum limit and I often find myself spurred by the momentum of the exercise into writing for much longer periods.

Sometimes when I am having a particularly hard time getting into the flow of my creative practice in the morning, I convert a spiritual practice into something I can use on the page. For example, I might use the meditation practice of *tonglen,* as taught by the American Buddhist nun and author Pema Chödrön. *Tonglen* is a practice of breathing in and sitting closer to those things we normally try to move away from because they are uncomfortable and breathing out and sending to others those things we habitually try to hang on to. I might take *tonglen* and adapt it to writing, repeatedly completing the phrases *I breathe in . . .* and *I breathe out* . . . Once, when an early morning flight made my prayer time at a hotel very brief, I sat in an airport and wrote my twenty-two prayers out on the page over three hours, each prayer opening to writing that flowed from the center of stillness amid the flurry of modern travelers.

I do my practice every day. This was not an instant process but one that developed only after fifteen years of periodically doing daily prayers and writing in my journal. For many years I would pray and write three or four times a week or every day for three months and then, inexplicably, stop. Even now, when I have not missed a day of practice in almost four years, I experience moments of resistance, of wanting to hurry through the prayers or cut short my time of writing in my journal. And when this feeling arises I sit and ask myself gently, *What is it you do not want to bring to consciousness? What do you not want to be with?* We cannot do our deepest creative work and remain disconnected from thoughts and feelings we find uncomfortable. Sometimes I truly have no idea what it is I want to avoid, but knowing the only way out is through, I begin writing by completing the phrase *I don't want to write about* . . . As uncomfortable as it can be to confront what I would prefer to outrun, after twenty years of doing my creative work as a practice, I know two things: that which we want to outrun will not lose its power over us until we can be with it; creative work will go deeper and contain more vibrancy if we stop trying to avoid something we do not want to face about the self or the world.

However you establish a way into your own creative work, creating rituals and routines that make it possible to begin when the wellspring of inspiration does not bubble forth spontaneously will help you do that work more often. A practice of any kind helps us be in the present moment, and this ensures that we will have the focus and energy needed to do our creative work. When we are fully present we experience our essential wholeness, the soul we are; and so we are not as likely to separate our spirituality, the awareness of the essence of life, or our sexuality, the awareness of the physicality of life within and around us, from our creativity. And so the creative work flows with the implicit insights and vitality these provide, offering something that feeds both other people and our own unfolding.

FOR CONTEMPLATION

- What if *how* your do you creative work, the attitude you begin with and the intent you hold, ripples out from you into the world regardless of the quality of the work you produce and whether or not the work you do is ever shared?

- What if establishing a regular practice of creative work really is the easiest way to do this work instead of relying upon your willpower and moments of inspiration to get started?

ESTABLISHING A CREATIVE PRACTICE

- Find a place to do your work. Experiment.

- If the spot is a room with other uses, try to locate it away from the place where you take care of daily logistics (bills, e-mails, phone calls, etc.).

- If you do your creative work when others are in your home, make sure the room has a door and that others understand the meaning of a closed door.

- Set up the space in a way that seems uncluttered *to you*. Be honest with yourself, and if there is mess that seems disturbing or distracting and if you are not good at organizing, get help!

- Decide how often you will do your creative practice. Start small. While a daily practice is wonderful, making an ambitious initial promise to yourself may simply set you up for discouraging failure. Make the initial commitment for regular intervals (daily, twice a week, weekly, twice a month, etc.) for a set period of time (for example, every day for this week or month; twice a month for the next three months).

- Decide on the timing of your practice. A practice is best done at the same time of day. Experiment with what is easiest for you to maintain before making a commitment. Try getting up an hour earlier. Try working before you go to bed. Try doing the practice on your lunch break. See what works.

- Do something physical before beginning your creative practice. Go for a walk, do some yoga or tai chi, some simple stretching or dancing. This will help ground your practice in the physical details of life.

- Decide on the length of each session of your creative practice. This may be done by designating an amount of work (five pages) or by setting a minimal time. Start small.

- Find a way to slow down and fully arrive in the place where you will work. Explore options from different spiritual traditions. Keep it simple. Small actions (taking three conscious breaths and letting your body relax, lighting a candle, etc.) done consciously and repeatedly at the beginning of each practice session will help you become ready to do your creative work.

- At the beginning of your practice, take a moment to set your intent for this session and to dedicate what you are doing to something larger than this moment. What purpose (in your life, in the world) do you hope your creative work will serve? It need not be grand or life changing. Just make it conscious.

- You may want to take a moment to mentally ask for assistance (from the muse, the unseen, the divine, the spirit of all writers or painters or composers everywhere) and offer your gratitude for this opportunity (the time, space, resources, and willingness) to creatively express yourself.

- Begin each session the same way. You could use one of a variety of warm-up exercises, record your dreams in words or sketches, write a story of something that happened the day before yesterday. Then go into working for the designated period.

- Keep working until the time is up, starting again and again if you get stuck or feel a piece is complete.

WRITING EXERCISES

- Complete each phrase repeatedly for the time allocated:

  I dedicate my writing (painting, composing, etc.) to . . .

  May my writing (painting, composing, etc.) serve . . .

  I don't want to write about . . .

  If it wasn't so risky I would write about . . .

  If I knew I could not fail I would . . .

- What would you do if you knew you had one year (or six months) to live?

- In the Buddhist meditation practice of *tonglen* we willingly sit with those things we usually pull away from (feelings of fear, worries about the future, physical discomfort, etc.) and mentally send out into the world with our breath those things we often want to hang on to (feelings of contentment, peace, joy, happiness, etc.). The practice is dedicated to alleviating suffering through the willingness to be with what is. It is done both for ourselves when we are suffering and for others, wherever they are, who are also suffering something similar. One of the feelings I often pull away from is tiredness and the fear that I will simply never be able to rest. When I write within the pattern of *tonglen* I try to open to concrete images, emblematic moments that hold the feelings I am trying to be with and send out. So I write,

I breathe in the blank stare of a bone-weary woman
riding the subway train at the end of the day.

I breathe out fresh daisies in a clear glass vase
Unexpectedly there on the kitchen table when she walks
   in the door.

Start with something, some feeling or thought or sensation you find uncomfortable, something you would normally pull away from, and open to images that carry the weight of what you want to avoid but now willingly sit close to, and write,

I breathe in . . .

And then, let the antidote, what would ease the difficulty in the first phrase, be similarly expressed in a sensory way by completing the phrase,

I breathe out . . .

seven

CREATING TOGETHER

One of the easiest ways to develop your creative work is to do it with other people. Writing, because it requires minimal space and equipment, is easily done with others, but years ago I both participated in and facilitated painting workshops where a dozen people worked separately, side by side in a large room. Perhaps more surprisingly, a friend of mine, experimental filmmaker Philip Hoffman, holds an annual Film Farm on his property outside Toronto. For ten years, experienced and neophyte filmmakers alike from all over the world have gathered for an intense week of filmmaking, each of them producing and sharing a short, hand-processed film within the container of the group's collective enthusiasm and experimentation. While some forms of creative expression, like theatrical performances, usually require working with others, and some others are easily done in a collective setting, all forms of creative work can benefit from and be adapted to working within a group.

Generally a small group (usually no more than a dozen) is ideal, but keeping our commitment to do our creative work can be made easier by agreeing to work with even one other person. The great gift of doing creative work with others is that the mutually agreed-to time and place increases your chances of showing up and doing the work. If you are wanting to do creative work but are finding it simply is not happening despite your best intentions, making an agreement to do the work at the same time and place as others similarly engaged is one of the easiest ways to get started and to develop a creative practice you may be able to pursue eventually on your own.

For years I facilitated a writing group that met in my home every second week for three hours in the evening. The group continued to meet after I stopped facilitating it, and after working out the slightly different logistics of running a peer group, they have continued to meet and write together. I will tell you here what I know from experience are effective ways of doing creative work within a group so that you, if you choose, can set one up yourself.

The first thing that needs to be decided in setting up a group is the process by which people come into the group. If you have the skills to facilitate a group and are putting out the word in a broad public way through mailings or advertising, then it will be up to you to screen potential candidates and, at least initially, decide who is in the group. The best way to screen people who are interested in the group is to ask them to tell you what they are hoping to gain from participation and to tell them how the group will work together. If your expectations meet, that person may be a good candidate for the group. If you are facilitating, it is your responsibility to see to it that agreements are clear and kept and that what is promised is delivered.

If, alternatively, you want to be part of a peer group, the initial setup could take longer. You may want to invite people you know and think would enjoy writing or painting or dancing or making music together for intermittent gatherings before you ask them to make any commitment to ongoing meetings. Once a peer group is established, new members need to be considered and approved by all current members. The ongoing peer group I mentioned above handles this by having people in the group suggest potential new members when there is room in the group. Any new candidate is invited to attend one or two sessions on a probationary basis, and then the whole group decides whether or not it feels like a good fit. In a peer group if even one person in the existing group is uncomfortable with a potential new member's participation, even if this person cannot or does not want to say why, the new person is not invited to join the group.

The groups I organized had several agreements that helped us do creative work. Everything that was shared within the group was confidential and not to be shared with others who were not in the group. We began and ended on time. We all did our creative work (writing, painting, etc.) continuously during the time designated for working and refrained from talking, wandering around, or doing anything else. People were free to share their work when time was available, but they had to ask for the feedback they wanted, and the feedback offered was confined to what was requested by the author of the piece.

With these agreements in place, a group can proceed to follow a practice of creative work that parallels the one I have described for individuals. Generally, after settling in, one person (the facilitator or a group member taking a turn) leads the group in establishing a container and a brief period of contemplation. This can be simple or elaborate but is best kept similar each time so that group members can benefit from a repetitive practice, which makes it progressively easier to slow down, be present, and find their way into doing the work. It may include a prayer or a meditation, the lighting of candles or incense, some singing or chanting. Keep it simple, unless everyone in the group is intimately familiar with the tradition drawn upon, so that group members will more quickly feel like co-creators of sacred space, space that is separate from and holds a different energy than the workplace or home from which they just came. Sitting in a circle helps to provide the sense of a container that includes everyone and to encourage mutual responsibility for the process.

After the opening, some form of introduction and establishing of intent helps knit the group together for the evening. One simple way to do this is to have each person say their name (even if all names are known) and one word or brief phrase (three or four words maximum) that articulates their intent for this time together. I encouraged people to simply sink down into the moment and speak the words that came from being fully present with themselves. The intent spoken sometimes surprised the speaker, often becoming clearer only after the creative work was done and sometimes remaining a mystery even then.

It's good to begin your creative work together with a warm-up, an exercise provided by either the ongoing facilitator or by a group member acting as facilitator for that evening. Together, in the circle, write or paint or move for a set period of time (usually ten to twenty minutes) using the warm-up exercise. At the end of this time, there can be a brief period for sharing the work that resulted. Generally no feedback is asked for or given on warm-up exercises, but the process serves to help everyone let go of expectations and move into the work. The real fun in sharing the pieces is in seeing how wide a variety of creative expressions can come from one common suggestion.

The group can then work for a previously agreed-to time. In the writing groups that met for a three-hour evening, we found a one-hour writing period worked and left enough time for opening exercises and some reading and feedback at the end. Often people moved about the house, sitting at a dining room or kitchen table or in comfortable chairs. Daylong painting sessions usually included two ninety-minute to three-hour blocks of time for working in a shared studio space. Other forms of creative work may necessitate individuals going off to different locations and returning after a set time. In all cases, the agreement is to keep working steadily for the designated time and to refrain from talking or doing anything else that might interrupt your work or distract others.

At the end of the time allocated for individual work within the group there is often a feeling of wanting and needing more time. Interestingly, when I facilitated weekend and weeklong writing retreats, members of the bimonthly group and I eagerly anticipated having longer periods of time in which to write. Much to our surprise, we found that three-hour blocks of time rarely resulted in more writing and sometimes did not produce as much on the page as those seemingly too short one-hour periods. Although we all sometimes fantasize about what we could do creatively if we had unlimited time, this experience illustrated to me how having a container where we can feel the edges and the slight pressure of real limitations can help sharpen our focus and keep us in the creative process.

After the period designated for doing your writing or painting or other form of creative work, the group can reassemble. Those who feel drawn to can share their work, although there may not be time for everyone to share at each gathering. In the writing and painting groups I facilitated, participants had to ask for the kind of feedback they wanted. I will say more in chapter 11 about receiving and dealing with others' reactions to your work, but for now I will say that I have always encouraged groups to be particularly gentle with work that has just been done in the preceding allocated time. Raw first drafts generally should not be critiqued instantly but rather responded to from the heart and gut with some tact and caring. Requiring that group members ask for the feedback they want and holding group members to that request ensures a level of safety that encourages the creative flow. A group that is doing creative work together is not a class, and members often lack skills for critiquing the technical aspects of the work. Often I would ask group members to simply sit or stand in silence as they heard or looked at another's work, sharing their reactions after a moment with a word or brief phrase *as their responses* and not as a critique of the work itself. However, as group members worked side by side over time, individuals would ask for specific feedback, wanting to know if some piece of writing required background information, had gotten sidetracked, or was unclear, sometimes seeking help with a particular problem. Often, when specific assistance was requested, the insights and help were readily available from the group.

The group's time together ends with opening the circle in some small ceremonial way, with a brief acknowledgment or prayer of gratitude for the shared time. As with individual practices, the group practice is easiest to maintain if it is simple and straightforward. Clearly, what is done in a group can be done with as few as two people. I have had many hours of fruitful creativity writing with just one other person and found that the time writing with others has reinforced my commitment to my private writing practice. One possible way to connect with others who are writing is online, through the Internet. My friend Peter Marmorek (who is responsible for the care and feeding of the oriahmountaindreamer Web site) has set up an online writer's community, called *Writers' Croft,* that uses some of the ideas talked about in this book. Peter is a retired English and world religions high school teacher who was part of the writers' groups I facilitated and at whose house the community has continued to meet. If you are interested in how an online community might work, you can have a look at the Web site at writerscroft.com.

Creative work is often solitary, but there can be a great sense of camaraderie and support when working in the company of others who share your commitment to the process. Shared silence is a gift too rarely found in our extroverted culture. Working in a group is one of the best ways I know to ensure that regular creative work takes place in the midst of a busy life. When the words on the page seem lifeless or the images that come do not inspire, if you are alone the inclination can be to give up and wander off to do something else. In those difficult moments the sound of other pens scratching out words on the page, the sight of others pausing, struggling, and continuing to put paint on paper or canvas and your commitment to the group can help you take a deep breath and begin again. Even if you do not have difficulty getting to or sticking with your creative work when you are on your own, working in a group can offer support and an opportunity to work in a different way. Sometimes writing in a group has helped me lighten up about my creative work. At other times the limited time frame and supportive atmosphere have

helped me go deeper and find the elusive thread of some writing
I will continue on my own later. One experienced full-time artist
who attended a painting workshop I facilitated was pleased and
surprised to find her work expanding in new directions when she
worked surrounded by fledgling artists. Working in a group container and seeing someone who has never written or painted before create and share a piece that amazes and moves them reminds
us of why we set out to do creative work in the first place, lets us
delight in the surprises and power of creativity. Working in a
group reminds us that humans are communal beings who co-
create the world they share.

FOR CONTEMPLATION

- What if getting to and continuing your creative work
  would be easier if you worked periodically with others
  similarly engaged? What if joining a group would simply
  be more fun and therefore a more sustainable way to do
  your creative work?

CREATING A GROUP

- Consider finding or starting a writing group. Be clear about
  all mutual agreements regarding

  —how people join the group
  —any minimum commitment to attend
  —confidentiality: what can and cannot be shared with
    those not in the group

—how and when work is shared in the group

—how and when feedback is offered

—how often, how long, and over what period of time
  the group meets

Establish a routine as a group that parallels the routine
for an individual practice (a way of beginning, setting intent, doing warm-ups, working for designated periods, and
ending).

WRITING EXERCISES FOR A GROUP

* Have everyone write the first sentence of a story on a piece
  of paper and put the pieces of paper in a bowl. Everyone
  draws one and writes a story beginning with the line they
  received.

* Have each person randomly name one object, and write
  them on a list. Give everyone ten minutes to compose a
  story using all the items the list. This can lead to great
  fun if people are willing to read their pieces. One group I
  facilitated came up with some surprisingly novel ways to
  incorporate *olive pitter* into each of the ten stories that were
  created. We then dubbed this exercise the Olive Pitter Exercise.

ADAPTING THE OLIVE PITTER EXERCISE
TO A VISUAL MEDIUM FOR A GROUP

- Peter Marmorek and Diana Meredith have adapted this
  writing exercise to creating computer collages. Each person
  in a group contributes one or more (depending on the size
  of the group) images to be used. Images may be their own
  digital photos, CDs of clip art, or downloaded pictures
  from a search engine. Then, within an agreed-to period of
  time (twenty to thirty minutes) each person creates a col-
  lage using all the images with an image manipulation program such as Photoshop. Because these programs allow for
  a wide array of changes to be made to images, the results
  vary widely. Of course, images taken from elsewhere are
  copyrighted and so the final results cannot be published,
  no matter how wonderfully they turn out. You could do
  something similar, although with a more limited range of
  changes, with glue and scissors and images cut out of magazines that have been photocopied to provide one of each
  image for every person in a group.

eight

A NECESSARY SILENCE

Monday was the day I had planned to begin this chapter, but I had a difficult time getting started. The reason was simple. After writing steadily last week, I spent Saturday at my computer updating my mailing list. Sunday, after searching online for places to stay on an upcoming trip, I talked with my sons, a friend, and my parents on the telephone and spent some time with my husband. It was a productive and enjoyable weekend, but it was too full. I did not leave enough empty time.

Empty time is time to lie in bed and contemplate dreams or the marks on the ceiling, time to go for an aimless walk or sit by the fire staring at the flames while pretending to read. Empty time is time to rest, renew, and replenish by following the impulse of the moment. Empty time is time to slow down, to find the stillness and spaciousness that allow us to stop all the doing and simply be. I know better. I cannot write for five days, do business for a day, and then stop to catch up on household details and with those around me and expect to dive back into writing. Oh, I did my practice in the morning, and I brought myself to my desk after prayer and yoga and writing in my journal, but I could feel a dryness within me. Deep inside I knew I would have to stop before I could continue.

But I didn't stop right away. I resisted. I dithered. I took a try at another chapter, made the car rental reservation for an upcoming trip, and took another stab at this chapter. Finally, since the snow had stopped coming down for the first time in days, I decided to drive to the post office in town and collect the mail. Drifting snow made driving precarious. I had to slow down and pay attention. Finally, I turned off the radio and just drove, watching for black ice and deep drifts, gazing at the land around me in the places where the pavement was bare and dry. The purple shadows on the snow covering the open fields draped the world around me in the silence I was finding so elusive. By the time I got home I was ready to surrender. I gave up trying to get something done, built a fire in the woodstove, and, putting Samuel Barber's *Adagio for Strings* on the CD player, I sat down and watched the light of the late afternoon drain from the pale winter sky.

If there is one consistent thing that stops people committed to doing creative work from doing it, it is this: a lack of necessary silence in their lives, an inability or unwillingness to find and stay with the stillness, to regularly create empty time in their day or their week. Too often I hear from those who have carefully set aside time in their busy lives for their creative work—an hour or two a day to write, a day a week to paint or compose—only to find themselves, despite a disciplined practice and consistent determination not to be distracted during the time set aside for creating, unable to follow the thread of creative desire that would take them more deeply into the process. Too often our days are filled with obligatory tasks, the sometimes minimal but necessary work of self-maintenance—getting enough sleep, sufficient exercise, and nutritious food—and taking care of our relationships with those around us. And then there are the chosen activities, the events that feed our creative impulses—the planned visit to an art exhibit, a play, or a movie. But if there is no time when absolutely nothing is expected or scheduled, we are not likely to arrive at the appointed hour ready to do our creative work. For as surely as a disciplined creative practice brings us to our creative work, so the spaciousness of empty time in our lives allows that which lights a fire within us—the muse, Buber's form, the creative impulse of the life force itself—to find and speak to us.

I know this as surely as I know I must breathe, and unlike many people, at this point in my life I have a great deal of control over my daily schedule. I am not living with children who demand constant attention, nor do I have a nine-to-five job. I cannot see my nearest neighbor, and I spend five days out of seven from early morning until well after sunset alone in a house surrounded by forest. And still I find it difficult to ensure that there is regular empty time in which to meander and find the stillness I know is so necessary to the creative process. This is evidence that although external circumstances can make setting aside empty time and finding stillness more or less difficult, the real struggle is an internal one. We are co-creators of a culture that equates who we are with what we do, that recognizes and values actions and accomplishments that can be observed and measured. The mystery of the creative process as a whole, and the elusive nature of that part of the process that is clearly not an act of will, that comes more from not-doing than doing, frightens us. We like to pretend it's not there, not necessary. Because if stillness and the fertile silence it provides are as necessary to the creative process as I experience them to be and yet cannot be attained by an act of will, then this process is not wholly within our control, not completely up to us. Knowing this, we face our own vulnerability, feel how dependent we are upon a grace we cannot name or understand to do our creative work, to live fully.

The paradox is that even though it is frightening to acknowledge that this vital component of the creative process is not within my control, not something I can make happen, it is what happens in the stillness that draws me to continue to write. When I ensure that there is empty time in my life and let myself meander until I come to some stillness in that time, the silence that finds me has a palpable presence beyond thought and words. And when I am willing to simply be with this presence, words and images and stories begin to flow and surprise me. It's these surprises, the things that come out on the page that I did not know when I sat down to write, that bring me again and again to writing.

We cannot begin our creative work if we do not have an idea of where we are going, the intent to write or paint or compose, and a practice that takes us into the process. But we cannot continue in a way that is faithful to the creative process unless, after beginning, we loosen our grip on the original idea and allow room for something else to happen, something that produces more than what we could produce from our knowledge and will alone. And we cannot let go, cannot surrender to the creative process itself, unless we can find some stillness and cultivate enough comfort with that stillness to allow ourselves to stay there where the creativity of a fertile and abiding emptiness can find us.

This may sound way too mystical for some, but the truth is that no matter what language we use to describe the inherently indescribably creative silence that sometimes visits us when we make ourselves available to it, our part in this process is very simple: we have to set aside and fiercely guard regular periods of empty time, time when we are not obligated or promised to anyone, any event or task or occasion, time when we allow ourselves to wander and follow the impulse of the moment. If the inspiration discussed in chapter 3 that gets us in the mood to create is the inhale, and the creative work itself is the exhale, empty time is the pause between the two, the place where we sit for a moment and wait for the impulse to take the next breath to come from a deep stillness. The quality of empty moments is that of an instance out of time, a moment of simply being. History is full of stories of creative solutions—artistic and scientific—that came to people not as they were poring over figures or doing more research or honing their technical skills, but as they were daydreaming in the bath or walking through the woods. There is something about leaving the process and doing nothing for a time that opens us, makes us available to something we miss if we develop myopic vision from having our noses pressed too closely and consistently to the grindstone.

Too often we have little sense of spaciousness in our lives. The sense of infinite potentiality into which I hope to dip my pen when I write is too often obscured with preconceived notions and anticipated outcomes, necessary planning and obligatory work. Even as we plan for time to do the creative work, we have to plan for empty time, deliberately create gaps in activity and planning and organizing, if it is to happen. And in a culture where few recognize the usefulness of empty time, where a person's worth is often seen as inversely proportional to the number of blank spaces in their day timer, we may have to devise strategies to ensure that misguided ambitions within or around us do not take over and put all our time to so-called productive use.

Years ago, I remember laughing out loud when I heard that M. Scott Peck, author of *The Road Less Traveled* and *People of the Lie,* had confessed in an interview that he spent the majority of what he called his daily "prayer time" wandering around daydreaming. He called it "prayer time" primarily to keep others from interrupting these periods of reverie with valuable tasks or meaningful social interaction. A year ago, reading Wayne Muller's book *Sabbath,* I discovered my own way of setting a boundary around the kind of empty time I need, against the inner and outer saboteurs of fertile idleness. When I call a day a sabbath, I inform both myself and others that this is a time when the usual measure of accomplishment does not apply, when I will not commit in advance to any task or goal or activity no matter how enticing but will simply follow the thread of desire that comes from the center of stillness. If that means I lie on the couch for hours watching the fire in the woodstove, that's okay. If it means I go for a walk but get distracted and don't go any farther than the pond, mesmerized by the dance of bugs skimming along on the water's surface, that's okay. It is a sabbath, a time of rest and renewal, a time to replenish, to connect deeply with a silence that is always there although often missed within me and the world. Calling it a sabbath, I recognize that to me it is sacred. This helps me guard against casually breaching the boundaries I have set and rushing back into everyday concerns or unconsciously responding to others' requests during this time I have set aside.

Of course, the mind is all too ready to fill empty time. Finding out what takes you further into and what draws you away from the ability to be still takes a willingness to honestly observe yourself. You have to try things and watch to see what helps you slow down, what increases and what diminishes your sense of an inner spaciousness. It's a process of trial and error, with most insights gained in hindsight. I have learned that if I feel drawn to, I can write in my journal on the day I have set aside as a sabbath, but getting on my computer to either write or surf the Net—as I did last weekend—speeds me up with too much information. Generally, apart from playing music I know will slow me down, I try to avoid the use of all electronic gadgets—TV, radio, telephones, computers—on these days of stillness. I may go for a drive, but I avoid getting groceries or doing errands. Lovemaking slows me down. Housecleaning speeds me up. Often, when it is warm enough, I go out into the woods and lie on the ground where the sunlight filters through the branches of the tall pines. This is the surest way for me to let all the noise, all the inner questions, list making, and mental preoccupations, subside. Sometimes I read or take a long bath or go for a walk with my husband and watch him take photographs of the patterns of light and shadow sweeping across the ground or through the trees. I still do my practice of prayer and meditation, but I often take much longer than usual, sometimes extending the practice into hours alone in the woods. And each time I find myself speeding up, each time I am tempted to get something accomplished, I think to myself, "This is a sabbath. Will this take me deeper into or further away from the silence I ache for?" I do ache for silence. Sometimes I feel I can't get still enough, can't find enough of the quiet I need to get out of the way of the creative work that calls me.

If you do not live alone, you may have to negotiate empty time, no matter what you call it. Of course you can enter a personal time of rest and creative renewal when others in your home are being industrious, but, as with writing, sharing this time with others—creating a mutual sabbath—can support your intention to slow down and find silence when you are tempted to give up and step back into the fray. Remember, however, that people find stillness in different ways. Jeff, my husband, is much better than I am at puttering, doing small jobs when they cross his mind and moving on to something else when he feels the impulse. Of course, sometimes on nonsabbath days when we have decided to get repairs around the house done, this can make Oriah-the-Focused a little crazy. Conversely, when we first started to designate certain days as a mutual sabbath, I was alarmed to see Jeff going off to work on these same small jobs. Repairing the screen door or touching up the paint on the baseboards in the kitchen would put me on the slippery slope of working through my endless list of all the tasks awaiting attention. This is because I have a mind that keeps endless lists and because I become easily attached to completion and outcomes. For Jeff, in part because he is not so attached to completion and in part because his nine-to-five job does not allow him much time to be at home, doing these small tasks at his own pace is relaxing, allows him to slow down and enjoy the present moment.

You have to find what works for you, what helps you slow down and touch a place of silence if only as small gaps in that ceaseless flow of inner chatter going on in most of us. Sometimes something unexpectedly helps move us from activity to receptivity, from doing to being. When we moved to the country about two hours outside Toronto, I knew that traveling would be less convenient. I could no longer hop in a cab and get to the airport or home from the airport in twenty minutes. Scheduling time to arrive at the airport when I was leaving town was no problem, but I dreaded the thought, after a long and exhausting week of travel, of catching a shuttle to my car and then driving for two hours to get home. But the reality of the experience was very different from what I had anticipated. Often I meet and speak with many people during a trip. Getting in my car and driving home proved to be a gentle and welcome transition from constant contact with others to solitude, from the rush and crush of urban areas to the spacious stillness of the countryside. I would get in my car at the airport and head northwest, often just as the sun was nearing the horizon. My body and mind would begin to slow down and relax as I drove farther and farther away from the city toward a horizon filled with dark silent trees silhouetted against a sky blazing with color. The drive turned out to be a gift, a transition that eased my way into stillness and the silence that could renew me.

Empty time is a necessary time of transition from doing to being, from acting exclusively with our will, often in response to others' needs and the world's schedule, to opening to the creative process, which has a different kind of rhythm, a flow that is not exclusively within our control, a movement that will take us to unexpected places. If I think of Martin Buber's proposal that art comes from a relationship between an *I* and a *Thou*, between an individual human consciousness and a form, a particular archetype of the Sacred Mystery, I see that part of what I bring to this exchange is the will and intent to do the work, the discipline and practice that get the work started and hopefully lead to the development of some skill in my chosen form of creative expression.

What is brought by the other, the *Thou,* the sacred and forever creative life force, is the opportunity to touch something larger than me, to be carried by a flow to unpredictable expressions of some truth or beauty I did not know before I began. To create in any form, we have to be willing to engage our intent and then let go and allow this grace, this flow, this unpredictable and some- times seemingly chaotic energy that is both what we are and yet larger than us, to direct the process. This is how our spirituality is not separable from our creativity.

I have never written a book, a poem, a story, or an essay that ended up being exactly what I thought it would be when I began. Sometimes the results have been almost diametrically op- posed to the idea that started the writing. In the winter of 2000 I sat down to write a new book. Having previously written a book about the deepest longings of the human soul, I wanted to write about how to live this longing, how to fulfill our soul's desires for deep intimacy with self, others, the world, and the Mystery. I started with a question: *Why am I so infrequently the person I really want to be?* I really wanted to find an answer. I wanted to know why, despite the clarity of my desire to live fully present and compassionately in the world, I often found myself distracted, disgruntled, and judgmental. And I didn't think I was alone in feeling that I often did not live up to my conscious, heartfelt in- tentions. I wrote seven chapters examining my life with a ruth- less honesty I hoped would lead to some insight that was helpful for both others and me.

And then I stopped and went to a retreat center. Frustrated by feeling no closer to answering my question, I decided to spend the first two days at this new location in meditative walking and sitting practices. I resisted the urge to keep writing. I turned away from the library of books that might have offered me insights written by others. I let myself wander. I walked down a long trail to a small lake on the property and sat and watched the birds. Slowing down, I felt my own tiredness. I went back to my cabin and took a nap. I had a leisurely shower. After eating dinner in communal silence, I helped wash the dishes and went to bed early. The second day flowed much like the first. I sat, I walked, I napped and watched and listened. I slowed down and found brief moments of real silence.

On the second night I had a dream. In the dream I saw one of the old women I have often seen in my sleep dreams, one of those I call the Grandmothers. Gently she said, "Wrong question, Oriah. The question is not why you are so infrequently the people you want to be, but why you so infrequently want to be the people you really are." She continued, "Because you have no faith that who you are is enough." Her voice was soft, full of sadness. "But it is. Your true nature as human beings is compassionate, and this essential nature makes you capable of being intimately and fully present. Who you really are is enough."

The next day I started at the beginning again, started to reconsider the whole thing from a different perspective, from the notion that perhaps the task was not to live up to some idealized standard, not to change who we are in some fundamental way, but to unfold and become who we already are in some essential way. The book I wrote was a very different book from the one I thought I was going to write. And, aside from a small and fleeting flash of irritation that the insight that changed my direction did not come before seven full chapters had been written, I did not regret any part of the process that led to the writing of the book as it is. I took myself to the process, something I could not have done if I had not had some intent and had not coupled this intent with the practice of writing regularly. Then I allowed myself empty time, time to wander and sit in stillness, time to let something else speak to me. And I listened. I let go of where I thought I was going to take the road the writing and the stillness had opened for me.

When I awoke after dreaming of the Grandmother's gentle but clear admonishment to reconsider the question I was asking in my writing, I was crying, filled with a sense of relief and gratitude that took my breath away. I felt I had come dangerously close to writing the "wrong" book, to writing a book that could have added to the grief we all feel at times about not being good enough, about failing too often to get it right, to love well. As always, my intent has been that what I write do no harm. The blessing of the creative process, the marriage of intent and grace—although no doubt primarily the latter—had made certain I did not.

The spiritual teacher Krishnamurti maintained that there was no path to truth. Creative work is always about accessing some piece of the truth, and so at some point it always requires that we leave the path, the well-worn patterns of activity and inquiry that make us feel safe. For many of us, for those of us who know how to work hard, be productive, and keep to a schedule, this can be the most difficult part of the process—finding and entering empty time. Start small. Set aside an hour at the beginning or end or even in the middle of your day, block it out on your day timer like you would an important business meeting, and then refuse to fill it in advance with something "worthwhile." Go for a walk and simply pay attention to yourself and the world around you. For the many years I lived in the city, a walk in a park or along a busy street, where I could simply walk in anonymity and watch life around me without being required to respond in any particular way, could slow me down and give me some empty time. Wander. I know how hard this can be. I remember the first time my husband took my older son, Brendan, out for a walk about three months after he was born. It was the first time I had been alone since Brendan's birth. I couldn't decide what to do. I lay down on the couch to read—a passion I had had little time or energy for in months—but then thought, "No, this is crazy! I should do some of the housework that is so hard to do with him here. I'll feel better if I clean up this mess." But minutes into cleaning I thought, "No. I shouldn't waste this precious time cleaning! I am so tired. I should have a nap." So I lay down. But my mind kept thinking of other ways to use this unexpected empty time. Needless to say, when my husband returned home with Brendan I had not relaxed, rested, gotten any work done, or had any fun. I had dithered the whole time away trying to decide how best to fill it. I had not yet developed any ability to sit still, to let the time be empty, moving only if and when the impulse to move came from a deep and renewing silence.

Some people wisely use their holidays as empty time, reminding me that the word *holiday* comes from *holy day*. What if we treated holidays as holy days, days set aside and held open to allow the sacred to enter and feed our hearts and souls, days to leave ourselves open to the creative impulse? Too often I hear of holiday plans involving activity schedules that make a normal work routine sound relaxing and open-ended. Most of us have to consciously make room for empty time and then learn how to follow the impulse that arises when we slow down and listen. I am learning to trust the fertile idleness that empty time offers and to keep a pen handy for the moments when something emerges from the silence and compels me to write. In those moments it is clear that I am simply a place in time and space where writing is happening. In those moments, to say I have the urge to write would be like saying that someone thrown off a high cliff now has the urge to fall. In those moments I am reminded of the Sri Ramakrishna's words, *Do not seek enlightenment unless you seek it as the man whose hair is on fire seeks the pond,* and I write as if my hair were on fire and the writing will take me to the pond. In those moments I am blessed.

FOR CONTEMPLATION

- What if empty time, time without plans, tasks, or scheduled events, is a necessary prerequisite for accessing your creative imagination, doing creative work?

- What if you thought of your holidays as holy days, time when you can be deeply touched and renewed by whatever comes when you are still? How might this change what you plan, where you go, what you do, and with whom you share these times?

CREATING AND BEING WITH NECESSARY SILENCE

- Schedule some empty time. Put it in your calendar. Make it an hour, two hours, or a half day, but schedule it regularly—daily, weekly, or monthly. Leave the time empty. Do not make any social commitments or any plans to do work or recreational activities in this time. Keep it empty.

- Label your empty time something that will help you keep it empty. Find a name that you and those of your social circle would consider inviolate. "Prayer time," "sabbath," "on retreat," or even simply "I have an appointment" might work (if you do not explain that your appointment is with yourself and stillness).

- Watch yourself without judgment. Notice what slows you down and what speeds you up. Notice what helps or hinders you in being still. Be honest with yourself, and notice under what circumstances you can simply sit or lie down or stand quietly watching without being caught up in reviewing the past or planning for the future.

- When you come to your scheduled empty time, sit still. It may take a while to become still. Be patient. Find the silence, and let all movement come from the impulse that arises when you simply sit and let your attention follow your breath. Use the things you know help slow you down and come to stillness. Avoid the things you know speed you up or distract you from being present. When you are in empty time and feel the impulse to move, ask yourself, "Will this take me away from or deeper into being quiet with myself?"

- Negotiate with those you are living with either for shared quiet time or for empty time when you can be alone. Explain to them your need for this time, and reassure them that it is not about leaving them physically or emotionally.

- Schedule and take empty time not only at the beginning of a creative project but also regularly throughout the process.

Let yourself sit with (not analyze or edit or think about)
the work you have done, opening to possible changes in
direction, letting go of your attachment to the work becoming what you thought it would be when you began.

WRITING EXERCISES

- Complete the phrase,

    If I had more time, I would . . .

- Assume that in the afterlife you will be allowed to keep one
  memory from this life and to live forever within it. Which
  memory would you choose? Describe it in vivid detail.

- Write a eulogy for yourself as if you had died today.

- Write a eulogy for yourself as if you had died at the age of
  one hundred.

nine

RISK AND SACRIFICE

My former father-in-law, Cyril, was a warmhearted, hard-working, slow-talking farmer. In the early fifties he and his young wife and their first son lived with his aging mother on the Prince Edward Island potato farm where he'd grown up. Then one night after his mother passed away, Cyril went to town and sold the farm for fifteen thousand dollars cash. It was hockey night at the local arena, so, much to his wife's consternation, he just tucked the roll of money into his jacket pocket and went to the rink to cheer for the home team. Within a month he and his wife had packed up their belongings and their two small sons and moved to Toronto, where he supported what was eventually a family of six by sweeping out the train station and sorting mail at the post office. For more than eighteen years Cyril worked shift work and never had a weekend off. When he died shortly after retiring at sixty, the doctor said the years of shift work had given him the body of an eighty-five-year-old.

Clearly Cyril's life was the stuff of stories, and he loved to tell them. But he wasn't good at it. I remember once, shortly before he died, asking Cyril how his recent monthlong trip to see relatives back east had gone. "Well," he said, pondering the question, "I left the house to go down and catch the train at Union Station about eight in the morning on a Tuesday." I loved Cyril, so I just smiled and settled in for a long and somewhat tedious account of thirty days of cross-country train travel and family visits.

An account of a series of events is not a story. A series of sounds or musical phrases is not a composition. Bits of color or shape, a string of images or random textures, do not make a piece of art. Cyril had the details but was missing the connective tissue that shapes a story. Once in a while I read a book that reports on real or imagined events with the same kind of plodding dedication to detail and chronology reminiscent of Cyril's accounts. "And then this happened. . . and then that happened . . . and then we went here . . . and then we went there. . . ." And I wonder what happened to the editing process, the process by which the raw material of stories—the words that are chosen, the real or imagined events that are described, the sensory details of inner responses and outer settings—are shaped and reshaped until they become something whole and complete.

In chapter 4 I described how seeing the world around and within us and discovering or creating interconnection between seemingly separate events stimulates our imaginations, offers us the raw material for the creative work we want to do. Awake to the world, we gather the materials we use: a phrase or word, an event or feeling, a color or the movement of light and shadow, a sound or taste or texture. I think of this process as finding the threads for the tapestry I weave as I write. For months before I begin to work on a specific project, my daily journal entries are a strange mix of recorded dreams, insights from moments of meditation, descriptions of things remembered or scenes in front of me, and ideas I think might fit into the upcoming book. Mixed in with margin notes on upcoming dental appointments and reminders to make arrangements to have firewood delivered are the ends of threads—ideas, thoughts, images, events—that may or may not be followed into a story in the upcoming writing. They are the places I can start when it is time to begin in earnest. It's not that the process of writing itself does not produce more raw material, but the accumulated threads of daily observations and ideas, particularly when I have had a specific writing project in the back of my mind, are the easiest places to start looking for what I want to say, to discover what wants to be written.

Others engaged in creative work similarly gather raw material. Before every show, which weaves a wholeness from the images he has captured and the music he composes, Jeff takes thousands of photographs and plays hundreds of variations of his music on the piano. My friend, filmmaker Mickey Lemle, records hours of footage before he creates a one-hour documentary. The painter stretches canvases, picks colors and brushes, takes photographs, and does sketches. The composer jots down musical phrases, themes, and possible arrangements. Carvers pick up bits of wood or cart home pieces of stone. And beneath all this physical gathering of the actual material we use to create, there is an inner collecting, a mulling of half-formed ideas, an intuitive reaching for the potential forms that live in invisible realms and beckon to us in the relationships between the stories and images, movements and sounds that cross our path. Those committed to ongoing creative work are always gathering materials that may be used in upcoming projects.

With our materials gathered, we begin the creative work of risk and sacrifice. Risk because we have to leave our habitual way of seeing if we are to see what can be made from what the world is offering us at this time. Risk because over and over again we have to let go of what we thought we would see or hear or feel to find the truth that is speaking to us, the story or image or movement or song that wants to be revealed by our creative work. Risk because when we do our creative work with this kind of openness—and it is the only creative work that interests me—we will be changed by the process, by what we learn about ourselves or our world, in ways we cannot predict. Risk because every time we arrive at the shore of a successfully completed piece of creative work, our feet on solid ground, hopefully feeling some inner sense of satisfaction, we have to leave that shore and venture forth again into unknown waters. Otherwise, we are simply repeating what we did before, and while that can be comforting to both us and those who like what we did before, it's not what creative work is about. To create we have to risk learning something, we have to risk shaking up our assumptions with a new way of seeing. And we have to risk failure. We have to risk falling short in our desire to convey in words, sounds, movement, shape, or color what our imagination has conjured while dancing with seen and unseen worlds. Sometimes we pirouette. Sometimes we fall flat. That's part of the risk.

And there is also sacrifice. Because any creative work involves choices—what to include or what to leave out, how to say or depict something—which automatically means other ways of saying or depicting it are ruled out. Our choices determine the structure and shape of the work, thus eliminating alternative structures and shapes. Often this begins with a process of being with and sifting through the raw material we have collected. Mickey views again and again the scenes he has shot, Jeff goes through piles of photos. The carver puts the stone or the wood in a place where he or she will see it often, pausing in daily tasks to watch the way the light hits the rough surface, looking for movement in what is solid.

When I begin a book, I start by going through all the writing I have done since the last major writing project. Sometimes, if the book is something I have had in the back of my mind for many years, I go through journals from many years ago, looking for the ends of threads that might belong to this new tapestry. And as I sift, I begin to collect and organize what seems to want to come along for this particular ride. I make notes on large sheets of manila flip-chart paper that I put up on the walls of my office with masking tape. I write those that seem to be connected in the same-colored ink, changing markers as themes change. In this way I begin to group ideas or bits of writing that appear related to particular themes and possible chapters or stories.

When we engage in creative work, we sit with and sift through the raw materials that have come into our hands and heart, hoping to find the movement, the flow of what has been speaking to each of us. We are hoping to see the shape and direction of what wants to be revealed, what we want to reveal, in this new piece of creative work. There is an inherent tension in this process. We could not start, could not even begin to gather materials, scenes, phrases, stories, images, or information, without some specific idea of where we want to go. But as we sift through all we have gathered, we have to let go of our attachment to that original necessary idea to see what is unfolding in front of us. Repeatedly, at each stage of the work, we have to proceed with an idea about the work and then let go of that idea to allow the creative process to unfold.

Filmmaker Mickey Lemle describes this process as learning to empty himself in order to find, release, and reveal the truth in the material he has collected. He starts with an idea for a film and begins to do his research, letting go of his ideas while talking to people in order to learn. He shoots hours of film with a new idea informed by the research he has done, and then he lets go of this idea as he reviews the footage, looking at it over and over, each time as if for the first time. And new ideas come and are surrendered to emptiness over and over as he finds the moments on film that speak to him. Holding in mind the ideas they have sparked, he rearranges scenes to find their relationship to each other, the way they might touch an audience seeing them for the first time. He searches for and creates the structure of the story, the shape of the film, as he goes, always letting go of where he thought he was going in order to allow the work to unfold.

If this all sounds chaotic, that's because it is—chaotic and intense. If I am to get a feeling for the underlying wholeness of what is there in my writing, I must stay with the process for extended periods of time over as many days as it takes to get through all the material I have accumulated. In the end I am surrounded with the colored threads of the book I am about to write, all the walls, windows, and doors covered with words in red and blue and green and purple, some linked with crooked black arrows, others highlighted with yellow asterisks or circled in orange. As I sit in the midst of this material, I am struck by the things that are repeated, the phrases or ideas that draw me immediately, make me want to make more notes or jot down ideas for stories next to them. I begin to feel the places where something is missing, as yet unknown. Usually I spend several days literally sitting with the words on the walls, rereading them, adding bits, gazing at the chaotic maze around me. Gradually I begin to make notes on a pad of paper, grouping ideas into tentative chapters, remembering stories that are hinted at, considering what has been left out. And over and over again, sitting in the midst of so much raw material, considering what to include, where to begin, what to expand upon, I ask myself, *What is the essence of what I want to say?* or *What calls to be said here?* Often when I begin I don't have an answer to these questions, or if I do my answers can change, as we saw in the last chapter, as the writing takes me deeper into the unknown. Like Mickey when he is making a film, I have to have an idea in order to start, and then I have to let go of where I thought that idea was going to lead, have to surrender to where the material and the process take me.

What I am describing here, my process of sorting through the raw material to find the wholeness in it, is one of an infinite number of ways to seek the shape of the piece you will create. Some people use tape recorders, dictating and then listening to their ideas in order to find out what does and does not belong in a particular creative work. Some carry small notebooks everywhere, jotting down ideas and images. Some never look at their notes while others refer to them repeatedly, and still others read through all their notes and then simply set them aside and begin writing or painting or composing, trusting that essential elements will remain while those that do not fit will simply not be remembered. Some allow room for trying a large number of options so they can discover all the ways a creative piece will not work, allowing themselves to make many mistakes, giving themselves the freedom to be a fool on the page or canvas, in rehearsal or on tape.

As with every other step of the process, you have to find your own way of discovering the shape of a particular creative work. But, however you sort the raw material of creativity, the process of discovery always contains certain elements. Beginning this process can feel a little overwhelming both because it is necessarily chaotic and because it requires that we stretch and, if only for a moment, hold all the possibilities before we make our creative choices. Then, in my experience, there is a point of creative critical mass, a place in the process where we fear that there will be no discernible wholeness, that no clear direction will emerge from the chaos of the bits and pieces before or within us. Often it is just after this time of feeling hopelessly lost, just after the moment when we are most strongly tempted to give up, that we begin to tentatively sense a beginning, the promise of a middle, the foreshadow of an end, begin to feel a vague underlying structure, some wholeness and meaning. There is a strange but seemingly necessary tension at this stage, a sense that although the way is not completely clear, the desperately desired release from the tension of chaos can be achieved only by diving in, by beginning in the place that calls to you. Of course, the more often this happens, the easier it is to have faith in the process, to immerse oneself in the chaos and allow the tension to build, trusting that the way will become clear. All that is required is a commitment to continuing and a trust in the process itself.

I don't mean to suggest that the process of finding a structure is always mysterious and difficult. Sometimes it is. At other times the whole piece comes at once, and it is all you can do to keep up with the movement, allowing one brushstroke or sentence to simply flow into another. At other times the way to proceed is made clear by discussing ideas or thinking out loud with others.

But, as in the later stage of reviewing and reshaping, the others from whom you receive ideas and feedback should be carefully and consciously chosen. Particularly at the initial stages of the process, I want to discuss my creative dilemmas and mental meandering only with those whose opinions I respect. Often they are people who have different creative outlets and so different ways of seeing. Sometimes they are other writers. But they are always individuals who refrain from quickly judging tender new ideas and tentative mental musings. Often I am aware that I am not so much seeking assistance as talking in order to hear myself talk, voicing my way through the chaos until I hear myself utter something that is clear and gives me direction. I urge you when doing creative work to talk with those whose ideas and ways of expression help you open to possibilities, and avoid sharing when you feel yourself tensing up or shutting down in response to others' input. And don't worry too much about why some people affect you one way or another. It may have nothing to do with them. Their tone of voice or mannerisms may unconsciously conjure childhood memories of a supportive and enthusiastic family member or a chastising third grade teacher. It doesn't matter why you react the way you do. Our commitment is to the creative work and to doing what will deepen and further that work, and so we share where the interaction serves this purpose. Generally, for me, there is a very small group—my sons, my husband, and a few close friends—with whom I sometimes discuss the process of finding the structure and underlying meaning, themes, and wholeness of a piece of writing. And even then I tend to do so only briefly, not wanting to muddy the waters of my inner process with too much input and too many opinions. But sometimes another's comment can be the catalyst that creates a critical shift in our perspective, allowing us to see something we have been missing.

At other times someone else's idea provides clear direction. One day someone who had read the prose poem "The Invitation" asked if I had ever thought of writing a book based on this piece. I had written a book eight years earlier and had accumulated a great deal of writing since that time, but I had been unable to find the structure for a new book amid all this collected writing. As soon as I heard the question, I knew that the prose poem was the structure for a new book, knew that many of the threads in the writing I had accumulated, if followed, would lead to an unfolding of each of the stanzas of the poem.

Sometimes the structure, the guiding principle by which you decide what to include and what to leave out, is provided just like that—as an unearned gift, grace. Other times you have to sweat it out alone, steeped in the juices of wanting to move forward and being unsure of where you are going, surrounded by the chaos of too many or too few seemingly unrelated bits and pieces. But this is the just the beginning. Choices that shape the work must be made continuously throughout the process.

Most often I begin with the loose outline I have developed from the material taped to my walls and write a first draft as quickly and steadily as possible. The momentum of steady creative work can carry us deeper into the process and bring us the surprises, the things we did not know before we began. Although I begin each day of writing by referring briefly to the outline and the notes I have made, I often do not consult these again until the end of the day, and sometimes I find when I do that the writing has gone in a different direction than I had anticipated or has unfolded in a way to make some of the pieces I thought to include unnecessary or irrelevant. Bits that have been left out that still seem alive to me I write on Post-It notes and stick to the outline for later chapters. Although I do not do any extensive editing until later, I do find myself often looping back through a chapter or a story as I am writing the first draft, reading it aloud to myself, rearranging passages and reaching again and again for the flow, the momentum that will carry me to what is next.

Again, this is a very individual process. I know writers who write the first draft of whole books without ever looking back or reviewing what they have written until they have come to some kind of ending. I have heard of composers and painters who spend hours or days in inner preparation and then write a complete song or paint a finished painting in one marathon session. Others build in layers, writing or painting the whole and then returning to redo and build upon, over and over, what was there before. Still others build each part of a creative work, perfecting each small piece before they go on to the next. One writer I know methodically writes and edits every sentence, going over and over each phrase until she feels it is right, before she goes on to the next sentence. An artist I know paints in fine detail, moving across the full length of the canvas one inch at a time with only the barest outline of the whole sketched onto the canvas.

There is no *right* way to discover the flow and wholeness of a piece. I offer these wide-ranging examples in part to emphasize this and in the hopes that you might consider experimenting with different ways of doing your creative work. I would find it hard to keep a sense of the whole, to stay connected to the overall flow of my writing, without reviewing and rearranging to some extent as I go along. And at the same time, I would become paralyzed and lose the flow completely if I labored over the structure of every sentence as it came. But different things work for different people. See what works for you, remembering that the definition of *works* is what enables you to do more of your creative work.

What I am describing here is the labor of creative work, through which we give birth to creative pieces. And, like any labor, it requires focus because focus, being fully here now, gives us access to the stamina and the resources we need to ensure a healthy offspring. Any distraction that takes me away from this moment, this movement of my hands across the computer keys as I lay down line by line the words and phrases of which writing is composed, makes the process more difficult and risks bringing the whole thing to a painful halt. I am speaking here not so much of the external distractions, which I dealt with in earlier chapters, but the internal ones: the voice of the critic, which says the work is no good or that the world simply does not need another book or song or painting or film; the voice of fear, which predicts failure at every turn; the voice of scarcity, which says there are only so many ideas and stories, cautioning me to hold something back, urging me to save something for later works. I know of no author, no artist, who has not encountered some version of these voices during the creative process. My response is simply to focus on the moment, on this breath, this sentence, to keep my mind fully engaged in the actual mental and physical process of composing and writing this line, allowing whatever comes to be written.

When the first draft of the book, the film, the show, the song is finished, when the first way of putting together the whole is done, set it aside and go do something else. Bake brownies, go to a ball game, shop, read a novel, catch up on movies, clean your closets. Try to leave the work alone for at least a week. Then go back to review and revise. Wherever possible, repeat this process two or three times, leaving the work alone for a time and returning to it again and again to revise.

Revising the work includes two processes: decisions about how to create the most powerful moments and flow throughout; and choices about what pieces need to be left behind and what pieces kept. When writing, I find the first process, the strengthening of sentences and paragraphs, the refining of a smooth, powerful, and coherent structure, relatively painless. I begin by reading whole chapters out loud. Problems with sentence structure, wording, and overall flow are much easier to spot when you can hear the text with your outer ear. Sometimes I come across organizational problems, places where things have been unnecessarily repeated or where the flow is interrupted. If it is not readily apparent how to remedy these problems, I read through the chapter and outline what I have written to discover just where the flow was lost and what needs to be cut, added, or rearranged to create or restore the continuity. Sometimes the problem is that a story or insight that simply does not belong has been inserted, and it has to go.

In his book *On Writing*, Stephen King, perhaps not surprisingly, urges writers to follow the admonishment of Sir Arthur Quiller-Couch to "Murder your darlings" when cutting out pieces that simply do not belong. And indeed it can feel like you are annihilating some of the children of your creative labors when you make the choice to cut a story, drop a scene, or leave behind certain movements, images, or musical phrases. When we cannot find a way to smoothly incorporate a piece we think is particularly well done or important, it is because it simply does not belong. And even if we could find a way to make it fit, we need to ask ourselves if it is our attachment to a particular piece, our reluctance to kill our darlings, that makes us want to include it. By the end of the first draft of a piece of writing, I have a clear idea of what I am trying to say, a sense of the essence of the poem or story or book. Choosing to keep or delete specific pieces has to be decided on the basis of whether or not they serve the essence of this particular creative work. If they do not, no matter how much it hurts to do so, they must be removed. When I finish a manuscript I have a file labeled "Unused Bits" filled with stories I have cut from the book. Although I have never used any of these pieces in subsequent books (and I don't rule out that possibility; it simply has not happened), they have popped up and been shared during some of my public talks, offering me some solace that they were not completely relegated to obscurity. Similarly, filmmakers often offer viewers much-loved but unused footage on the DVD editions of their films.

There is a limit to how much you can edit your own material. When I find myself going over a choice again and again, I err on the side of leaving it as it is so that I can get the perspective and feedback of another. The author of a work is sometimes simply too close to the work to see ways to make it stronger, clearer, or more powerful. Some pieces of writing require extensive editing by another, others require very little, but all writing that is to be shared needs to be edited by someone else, hopefully by someone with a commitment to the work and with good editing skills. A writer has to have confidence in the skills and intent of his or her editor. I have met a number of writers who express anxiety about being published by others for fear that the editorial process will transform their work into something very different from what they had intended, something that does not feel like their own. This has never been my experience. I start from the assumption that the editor is interested in making my book the best possible book it can be. And I can almost always see how the editor's suggested changes do just that. Often an editor is able to remedy problems I simply could not find a way around or point to places where there is a difficulty I could not see. On the rare occasion when I disagreed with an editorial suggestion—I am thinking now of one editor's suggestion that I replace the word *seduce* with the word *entice* to avoid the sexual implications of the former—I explained the reason for my choice (I wanted to imply the juicy overtones of seduce and was willing to risk making the reader squirm just a little), and my choice was left standing.

Of course, other people besides professional editors may be able to help you decide what needs to be sacrificed. Because my first book was about the shamanic practices I had learned, I asked several people who were interested in but not familiar with the subject to read the manuscript and tell me if they found the material understandable, clear, and accessible. Their feedback as potential readers was valuable. Later, I gave an early version of another manuscript to four people whose opinions and perspectives I respect. Much to my surprise, their feedback was contradictory. One wanted more stories, while another wanted fewer. One highlighted how a particular story had touched him deeply with its authenticity, while another targeted the same story as being suspect and less powerful than others.

I learned something valuable from this. All feedback is subjective and may be telling you more about the observer than about the work itself. If different observers you respect give you similar feedback about a specific passage or an aspect of an unfinished work that needs to be changed in a particular way, revise. If you get contradictory feedback about the work or a particular passage, revisit it with these comments in mind but do not try to keep everyone happy. The bottom line is that you as the author of the work are responsible for the risks you take and sacrifices you make. When that work goes out into the world, you need to feel that it is the very best of what you have to offer at this time. And then you need to let it go.

Letting go is easier if you have given all you have to give to your creative work, if you have not shied away from making necessary sacrifices or taking required risks. Although all that I thought to include in a book may or may not find a place in its pages, I do not keep stories or ideas in reserve, hoping to save them for some future publication. Holding back because you are worried about others' reactions or concerned there will not be anything left to say never serves the creative process. Holding back for any reason always produces a work tainted with the taste of fear. Committing to our creative work requires faith in the process's ability to carry us, to provide what we need in our work when we need it, now and in the future. At the end of every book I have written, I felt that I had said all that I could possibly say, all that I knew. Even when I had made an agreement to write another book, I did not hold anything back for anticipated future writing. I spent it all—all my energy, my ideas, my stories—on the creative work I was doing in the present. And when I was emptied, I sat still and waited. I won't tell you that it didn't make me nervous. I wondered if I would be able to write another book, if I would ever have anything more to say. But I went about the business of daily living, taking notes, writing in my journal, doing my practice, and paying attention. And the world and life filled me again, offered me new insights, new questions, new stories. At the end of the prose poem "The Call" I wrote,

Remember, there is one word you are here to say with your whole being.
When it finds you, give your life to it. Don't be tight-lipped and stingy.
Spend yourself completely on the saying.

This is how I want to live, so it is how I want to do my creative work. And to a large extent it is the open-ended, self-renewing, and ever-expanding nature of the creative process—of creation itself—that is teaching me how to live this way, how to trust the underlying and imminent life force that sustains us all. And my faith sends out roots, grows stronger, deeper. I sometimes think of writing the first draft as accumulating clay for a sculpture. But it is the sacrifice, the editing, the choices about what to leave and what to carve away, that creates the sculpture. Otherwise I'd just have a pile of mud. How we do our creative work, whether or not we make conscious choices, whether or not we allow the wisdom of inner and outer worlds to guide us, whether we hold back or risk everything for a truth that will sustain us, is how we live our lives.

FOR CONTEMPLATION

- What if all creative work involves risk and sacrifice? How comfortable are you with risk and sacrifice in your life? Where do you find it difficult to take risks? Where do you find it difficult to make choices, sacrificing some possibilities?

- What if the creative process necessitates periods of chaos, times of feeling lost, of being surrounded by potential material for creating with no sense of how to find any direction or wholeness within the multitude of bits and pieces? How do you deal with chaos in your life? How do you handle being lost?

SHAPING THE WORK

- Find a way to look at all the bits and pieces of the creative project you are working on right now. Reread your rough writing and notes, review your journals, listen to taped notes, listen to your music, look at the images you have created over and over. Try to be with all of the incomplete bits and pieces that you have right now.

- If it helps, talk with others about the material, the insights, ideas, images that have come to you with regard to a particular piece of creative work. Choose whom you speak to on the basis of how you feel when you converse with different people. Does talking with a particular person open you to seeing differently, to considering new possibilities, or does it close you down, make you cautious, hesitant?

- As you look at the material, ask yourself, *What is the essence of what I want to say? What calls to be said here?* Let the answers to these questions bubble up from the material itself.

- Experiment with different ways of writing or editing and see what works, what leads to more writing. When do rereading, rewriting, and editing what has been written or photographed or composed (after an hour, a half day, a day, a week) help maintain the continuity and momentum, and when do they simply postpone doing the writing? Use what works to keep you writing.

- After completing the first draft of a piece, put it aside for at least several days or a week. Do other things: go for walks, reorganize your spice cupboard, make soup, visit neglected friends or relatives. Then come back and revisit the entire piece.

- Ask yourself questions as you review. *Is this the most powerful way I can say or depict what I want to say, what needs to be said? Is this really true? Is this something I know or imagine or hope to be true? Is this the whole truth? Am I hedging at all? What am I holding back? What don't I want to include, to leave out? What am I refusing to risk?*

- Consider the flow, the coherence and unfolding of each piece and the whole. Can it be made better? Can it be changed to more powerfully carry the receptive beholder deeper into the work?

- When you find problems with the flow or organization of the work, write an outline by going through the whole piece, and notice where something may be missing or where something appears that simply does not belong.

- If something—a phrase, story, image, metaphor—does not belong, take it out. If in doubt (or resistant), ask yourself, *Does this belong here? Does it add anything to what is being said? Is it necessary? Does it serve the overall purpose of the piece in an essential way?*

- Find a skilled editor you trust, someone you know wants to make the piece better and has the skills to do so. Be open to the changes he or she suggests. Resist only where a change would alter something essential that cannot be sacrificed.

- Offer the work to others, and specify what kind of feedback (content, flow, coherence, impact, etc.) you want.

- Remember that all responses are subjective. Consider each response (and consider similar responses from different people particularly seriously), but understand that choices about any changes to be made are yours.

WRITING EXERCISES

- Complete the following phrase repeatedly:

  When I feel lost I . . .

- Imagine you are an elder giving advice to a young man or woman about what to do when they are physically lost. Tell them what they should do.

- Tell a lie as if it were true, with convincingly intimate sensory details about

  —who you are

  —what you do for a living

  —where you live

  —your family background

—why you are in this writing group.

(This is a great writing exercise for the first meeting of a writing group, and having members share their pieces is both fun and often surprisingly revealing.)

ten

THE ARTIST'S LIFE

Years ago, when I read Natalie Goldberg's book *Writing Down the Bones,* I was drawn to her account of writing in cafés. Something about the idea of a woman writing surrounded by other people coming and going, a solitary rock sitting still while the stream of a busy day's activity flowed around her, appealed to my imagination. So I took my journal and headed for the nearest neighborhood coffee shop. But it didn't work for me. I became distracted by the people around me, felt compelled to jump up to hold the door for the woman pushing a stroller, was pulled into a conversation about the weather with the retired security guard who ate breakfast there every day. On those rare occasions when I found the writing beginning to flow, I wanted to get home to my computer as quickly as possible so my fingers could keep up with the words as they came. The number of people coming into the café who stopped and asked me what I was writing did not en-courage me to take my laptop and provide these inquisitive minds with the chance to read over my shoulder.

Writing in cafés works for Natalie Goldberg. For her, it's a practical part of a creative process that produces powerful writing. For me, it was an appealing idea consistent with some vague notion I had about a writer's life. We all have ideas about the artist's life, the life of the poet, painter, composer, performer, sculptor. I don't know where these ideas come from—probably the movies—but they rarely include scenes of the writer cleaning the oven, the sculptor nursing a sick child all night, the composer doing laundry, or the painter weighing the merits of various long-distance telephone plans in order to get the best deal. But of course the lives of artists are first and foremost human lives. The trick to ensuring that our creative work is not left by the wayside amid the daily logistics of a human life is to leave the fantasies behind and integrate our creative work into our daily lives.

There are two critical aspects to cultivating a life that supports and encourages the creative work you want to do: an honest assessment of your own human frailties—the ways you are most likely to be derailed in the creative process—and a plan for how to ease your way around them; and the creation of a community of support, relationships that continually midwife you in the creative process.

Creativity flourishes when we combine open, empty fertile times with regular periods of focused intent and disciplined work. But different personalities come to the process with different strengths and weaknesses and so need to consciously create these two in different proportions. I have little trouble taking myself to a committed time and place to do a daily practice that includes writing. Similarly, when I am working on an ongoing project I take myself to the computer every day with relative ease. But this natural ability for discipline can and often does slide into a kind of drivenness, a tendency to fill every moment with productive, goal-oriented activity. And creativity cannot thrive on disciplined activity alone, needs time to breath, to lie fallow, to daydream and wander. Knowing my own propensity for focused productivity, I have to consciously put myself in surroundings that encourage me to slow down. I have to consciously leave empty time in my day and my week and hold a boundary around it against my own inner drivenness or the world's urging to do more.

And just as being disciplined is not the same thing as being driven, neither is providing fertile, empty space the same thing as falling into total inactivity or numbing out by visiting the casino slot machines or watching endless television. If you know that your struggle is to get to the actual work, if you know your propensity is to procrastinate, you must surround yourself with what encourages you in a regular practice of creative work, what gets you to pick up the pen or paintbrush even when you do not feel like it.

Honestly evaluating both what you need and what works for you in keeping this balance can be a tricky business. Just as disciplined work and driven productivity can look a lot alike from the outside, so too can procrastinating and sitting in empty time seeking energy and inspiration for creativity. There is no point in lying to yourself. You may be able to fool others, but if you are committed to your creative work, you will find the strength to be honest with yourself about whether or not you are finding the mix of disciplined activity and empty space that you need in order to do your creative work. If in doubt, there is only one real litmus test: Are you doing the creative work you ache for? An honest answer to this question will be easier to find if you can refrain from making moral judgments about your strengths and weaknesses. I see the personality traits I have as similar to the physical characteristics I have inherited and developed over a lifetime—as simply the stuff I have to work with. I will probably always be inclined to work too much, to leave too little time for the necessary silence and fertile emptiness that writing requires. After many years of judging myself as lacking because of this, after years of hoping to wake up one morning with a different, gentler, less driven personality, I now accept that this is simply what is. Drivenness is not what I am. It is a characteristic that arises in the personality I have to work with somewhat more frequently than it might in other personalities. Accepting this, I am freed from the shame that makes it hard to be conscious when this aspect of my personality is running my day. Without this awareness of what is, I will find it impossible to make choices that shape my day in another direction, in a direction that provides me with what I need to write the way I ache to write. There are, of course, other personality traits besides a propensity to be driven or to procrastinate that contribute to what we need in order to do our creative work. What I am advocating here is a gentle, ongoing evaluation of your personality's tendencies, characteristics, strengths, and weaknesses to help you consciously create a life that will support you in your creative work, the life that is for you the artist's life.

A human life is made up essentially of meaningful work and intimate relationships. Whether you receive an income from your creative work or are financially supported to do it by another means, it is at least a part of the meaningful work you are here to do in this lifetime. Cultivating an artist's life, a life that supports this meaningful work, is largely about creating relationships with yourself, others, and the world that support that work.

All creative work requires some degree of solitude. We have to know ourselves and have access to our inner world if we are to have anything to bring to the work. Some forms of creative work, like writing, are largely done alone and necessitate a lot of solitude. This fact is one of the things that both attracts and frightens me about the process. I can honestly say that I never feel lonely when I am writing. As my fingers move over the keyboard, as my pen glides over the page, I become more deeply aware of both myself and the larger wholeness, not as an idea but as an experience of belonging to and cocreating that larger reality. Although I am alone when I write, I often feel less separated from the world and from the Sacred Mystery that runs through it all than I sometimes do when I am with others.

But I cannot write all the time. And sometimes, when I come out of a period of writing intensely, of seeing or communicating with only my immediate family, I fear that there will simply be no social life to return to, that my social relations will have withered and died from neglect. I think my fear about this comes in part from my enjoyment of the solitude. I struggle to accept that although I value others I really do not feel the need to socialize frequently or in many of the ways that are considered normal in my culture. But some small part of me thinks I *should*. I am reminded of my high school years, when I walked between classes often working on some story or line of a poem in my head. Preoccupied with my inner process, sometimes jotting down notes as I walked, I often did not look for or find fellow students who were going my way, did not bother to ensure I was walking with others. My brother, a year younger than me, remarked to me once that others saw me as aloof and unfriendly because I often walked alone and did not seem concerned about finding a group where I could belong. Like most teenagers, I wanted to be liked, did not want to be seen as antisocial, and I worried about what my brother had told me. But, despite my desire for a social life, I was more interested in both my internal world and the bigger world outside my school and small town than I was in the world of teenage angst, where you could be judged for walking to class alone. I thought I should make an effort to link up with a group between classes, but I just couldn't be bothered expending the energy.

I suppose it is somewhat similar for me today. Some voice of social etiquette says I *should* be more social than I am, *should* spend more time cultivating social relationships and participating in social occasions. My friend, author Jennifer Louden, says that the word *should* "is always a dead giveaway we are pushing ourselves out of our center and toward the outside world's dictates." Socializing is just not where the majority of my energy wants to go. I want to write, and writing is done alone. I am not extolling the virtues of social isolation. We need other people in our lives. However, the image the mass media often presents of the good life as including large circles of seemingly intimate friends, even if it is possible, may not be desirable for some of us. I need a great deal of solitude for both my creative work and my happiness.

More important than the quantity of time we spend on our social relationships is the quality of those relationships. And there are times when, worried about our ability to do our creative work, we may unconsciously cultivate relationships that ensure we do not have the time or energy to get to that work and see what we could do. Sometimes it is easier to make ourselves available to others who seem to need never-ending support than it is to make ourselves available for the creative work we fear will never come to fruition. Sometimes a friend with a flair for ongoing drama can provide a welcome distraction and give us an excuse for not giving our all to the work that calls us. Recognizing our own propensity to use others as a way of avoiding our creative work and then letting go of these relationships because they are neither fair to the other nor good for us can be a painful but necessary step in living more consciously and doing our creative work.

I think of the friends I have now and see that many of them are individuals deeply interested in, sometimes struggling with, but always committed to their own creative process in a variety of forms. Seeing and hearing how others find ways to weave access to inspiration and time for creative expression into their busy lives supports and inspires me to do the same. My dear friend Philomene Hoffman's commitment to her musical composition and performance, a commitment that has reduced her income and developed her talent greatly over the past ten years, is an inspiration to use my time well and remember what matters. My friends Peter and Diana (originators of the glue art mentioned in chapter 3) provide constant reminders to find new ways to foster creative inspiration alone and together. They plan regular art dates with each other. Together they go out to locations that appeal to them both, where Peter takes photographs while Diana sketches. Later they share their work and delight in how they saw things in similar or different ways.

Many of my closest friends—and they are a small circle of the family chosen by the heart—are artists in their own way, each of them, with varied degrees of success, continually searching for and finding ways to make room in their lives for creative expression. I did not consciously choose these friends because they were involved in creative work, but we were drawn together and able to sustain our relationships over many years in part because we share a commitment to finding ways to express the creativity we ache for.

I am not suggesting that if you want to do creative work, everyone in your life must be an artist of one sort or another. But we need the solace and support of those who know about the rewards and challenges of doing creative work. It helps us continue. And while everyone in my life does not need to know this process from the inside out, I shy away from spending any of the limited time I have with those who seem to actively want to undermine the desire to create, those who, for their own reasons, would discourage me from returning to the writing I love. At this point in my life this process happens quite naturally. I am drawn almost unconsciously to those who value and offer mutual support for creative work, and I do not feel the desire to spend time or energy with those who devalue or denigrate it. But when I was younger, when I first started to recognize that writing was something I wanted to make a priority in my life, I had to consciously let go of some of the relationships in my life if I was going to continue to write. In hindsight I can see that most of those who questioned my "crazy" need to write, those who urged me to do something that had some hope of improving my economic situation or contributing something of "real" value to the world, were primarily those who had given up on following their own creative desires years before. When we have surrendered something our soul wanted us to hold close, the pain is often so great that we have to believe that we had no choice. Being close to someone who makes a different choice can make it hard to maintain the illusion that we had to give up on our dreams, our longing to write or paint or dance, to play music or tell stories. Sometimes when I think now of the woman who called my desire to write stories "childish" or when I think of the man who admonished me to give up the "self-indulgence" of writing and get an education in something that would actually make a difference in the world—something like law or medicine or business—I feel a great sadness for whatever dreams those individuals left behind. And I know that the choice I made to move away from these relationships, from these voices of doubt and fear at a time when my own doubts and fears were threatening to bury my commitment to creativity, was a difficult but wise one.

Dealing with the voices of discouragement is much more difficult when those voices belong to the members of our immediate family—to our spouse, our children, or our parents. In this I have been very fortunate. Many years ago, teaching classes at night and writing in the daytime, I remember standing in my kitchen pondering my small family's financial future. Making barely enough for my sons and me to live on, I was considering an unexpected job opportunity. A well-meaning friend, someone who had given up his writing to go and work in the high-tech field, had called and told me about a job he thought he could help me get at his workplace, a job where I would be working forty to fifty hours a week and making five times the amount I was currently earning. Leaning my forehead on the cool glass of the kitchen window, looking at the dirt-encrusted snow in the courtyard outside, I spoke out loud just as my sons, then thirteen and sixteen years old, came into the room.

"Maybe I should just go take the job. We'd have paid holidays! We'd have a dental plan! And we wouldn't have to try and figure out how to scrape together enough money for every little thing that came along."

My sons spoke almost in unison, shocking me with the speed and vehemence of their replies. "No!"

"We have everything we need."

"We don't need fancy vacations or anything else."

"You're good at what you do, and you offer something to people."

"We're doing fine."

"You can't quit!"

I felt like their voices woke me up, snapped me out of some trance in which I was at risk of forgetting what mattered.

I don't mean to suggest here that the choices that support our creative work will always entail decisions to turn down well-paying jobs. But the inner and outer voices telling us that we should give priority to financial security, that our happiness is dependent upon a larger or more secure income, vastly outnumber the voices telling us to consider what would be best for continuing and deepening our creative work. Sometimes, doing a job that frees us from worry about providing for ourselves or those we love provides us with an essential ingredient needed to pursue and enjoy our creative endeavors. My husband, Jeff, spent several years living off the money he made playing piano in bars and restaurants. Not only did he have to adopt a standard of living he found oppressive, he rarely got to play the music that he most loved. So he got a job he enjoys, a job that has its own creative challenges and provides him with an adequate income designing the circuit boards that run computers. And he tends to his musical impulse by playing bassoon in a community band, composing at home, and playing for friends and at his own photography shows. This works for him. I have known more than one artist whose employment came too close to their creative work to leave them with any energy or inclination to pursue their creative expression at the end of the day. If you spend eight hours a day writing technical manuals or composing advertising jingles, you may not feel like you want to sit down to work on your novel or compose your own music when you get home in the evening.

Again, you have to try things and evaluate what works for you. For me, being self-employed teaching classes on spirituality kept me in touch with my deeper self and gave me the time and flexibility I needed to write every day. This was more important to me and my creative work than a higher or more secure income. I was more grateful to my sons than I could express for reminding me of this on a day when it looked like it might just be easier to forget all about the writing.

The people who love us want us to be happy. If they are having a hard time supporting us in our efforts to do our creative work, it is possible that we have not communicated to them how important this work is to us. It is possible that they are afraid our creative work will take us away from them. It is possible that they have left behind some of their own creative impulses and unconsciously resent being asked to support someone in making a different choice. It is possible that beyond assisting in the provision of concrete resources—a room in which to work, a regular time alone, resources to buy supplies—they simply don't know what we need from them, don't know how to support us.

Life is messy, and nowhere is this more true than in intimate relationships. I have heard many stories about women and men who felt they had to choose between caring for their families and doing their creative work. But it is an impossible choice, a false dichotomy, because loving the world and loving ourselves are just two sides of the same indivisible coin. I think some part of me once feared that if I went too deeply into the writing it might require a solitude that would take me from my sons. But eventually, as I wrote, I realized that the creative impulse that called to me, the kind of creative heat that makes me ache to pick up a pen, makes another long to move with the music or shape clay with their hands, always serves life. And life would not be served if the children were abandoned or all our friends and lovers were cast aside. Our creativity is not separable from that which feeds body and soul, from the needs and pleasures of living a physical life in a human form that requires relationship with others. The demands of small children are real, and creative work may go slower during the child-rearing years. But all artists' lives are deeply embedded in the living and longing of a human body and heart.

Sometimes, especially if you are starting creative work after years of not doing it, and if moving in that direction creates changes in your family's household or schedule, it may take a while before everyone can get on board and actively support your need to do creative work. Although I do not believe you can live indefinitely in intimate relationships with people who do not see and appreciate the creative work that is closest to your heart, sometimes it takes time for them to be able to do this. How much time is enough is again something you will have to decide for yourself. Patience is not my forte. What I do know is that you can make this process easier for yourself and for your family if you seek out support elsewhere, if you do not expect your family to be the sole provider of encouragement and support for your creative work.

Many years ago I listened as a workshop instructor emphasized how important his relationships with other artists were in sustaining him in his creative work. All of his stories were peppered with the names of other artists—writers, painters, performers, musicians—some of them known, many of them unknown, but all of them actively engaged in their own creative work and participating in a camaraderie of mutual support. I was overcome with envy. Full of self-pity, I remember thinking, "Well, that's just great, but I don't know anyone who does this kind of thing! I am alone. How would I ever meet people like this?" It was a reasonable question. At the time I was a single mother with two small children working full-time facilitating groups at a community mental health agency.

Relationships take time. Communities are built over years. Finding others who share your interest and understand the rewards and challenges of creative work is a slow process, and one best seen as both an end in itself for the joy it brings and a by-product of doing the work. A community of support is built so we can give and receive support for creative work. If we want to do creative work in the hopes of meeting and being included in social circles of people we think will be more interesting or valuable than others because they are "artists," we will end up in trouble. I can think of several people I know who, usually by providing necessary equipment and space for others who share the mode of creative expression they claim as their own, have managed to establish at least temporary relationships with other artists while doing little or none of their own creative work. But eventually those who are fully engaged in the process want to talk with others who are similarly engaged, and those who are actually doing the work can tell pretty quickly when someone else is not, when someone is more interested in being a writer than in actually writing, in being a musician than in actually doing the work of composing or developing the skill to play instruments.

The truth is that the more you engage in your creative work, the more you will find yourself surrounded by others who are similarly engaged. Of course, there is nothing wrong with deliberately going to places where this might happen. Reading poetry at an open mike in your local community may be more likely to put you in touch with those who are interested and engaged in similar writing than does publishing a chapbook of poems. One of the ways to find other writers or artists is to enroll in a course aimed at teaching the skills involved. A good teacher, class, or workshop is one that gets you to do more creative work. This means that some teachers will work for some people and not others. Investigate. If at all possible, talk to the instructor before you enroll. Ask about the in-class process, how the creative work is done or presented, the way feedback is handled, and evaluate whether or not it will suit your way of working. Consider your strengths and weaknesses. What do you need? Are you looking for a structured way to ensure that a period of creative work happens in your life each week, or do you want a critique of your work? Of course, often it is only clear once you are in a program whether or not it will work to get you doing more of your creative work, and if you are finding a group or class or workshop is killing your desire to do the work, is resulting in your doing less work, leave!

Similarly, you may be able to meet writers or artists at residential retreats and workshops, although in all honesty I have to say that this has worked only occasionally for me and for many others I know. The difficulty is that people come to retreats and workshops with very different and sometimes unconscious or secret agendas. I say this as someone who has been both a facilitator and a participant at writing and painting retreats. No matter how clear the process has been outlined in advance, some people come primarily to do the creative work while others come primarily to socialize. The difficulty, of course, is that the socializing can and often does interfere with the creative work far more than the reverse. This can be true in both a practical sense, as when late-night parties in shared residences make sleep impossible, and in a less clear but still powerful way when a group has mixed agendas. When your desire to do creative work is not supported but is rather tested by others moving in and out of the process and calling to you to join them in their revelry, it can be hard to find the resolve to continue. If the work is feeling difficult, a well-timed invitation to quit is sometimes all it takes to derail the process. Unless the facilitator is very good at holding the group to the task of doing the creative work, the socializing tends to take over. And in all fairness to facilitators, it is very difficult to motivate people who want to party to do otherwise. I have seen more than a few individuals in this kind of setting frustrated in their hopes of getting some writing or painting done after expending a great deal of time, energy, and money making all the arrangements necessary to get a precious two weeks away from work and family commitments. While these settings may meet your needs to find and connect with others involved in creative work, be sure to ask lots of questions before signing up. If the structure is loose and the intent is ambiguous, the retreat may not even attract people who are really engaged in doing creative work, may attract primarily those who want to be writers or artists but don't actually want to do creative work. A schedule that includes daily periods of shared quiet or silence and mutually agreed-to times for doing the work and a situation where participants are unable or are asked not to leave the site to go to the local pub in town every night increase the chances of actually doing some creative work at the retreat. When a retreat really allows, supports, and challenges participants to take their work deeper, the bond between those who attend is often lifelong and heartfelt.

Some of the writers and artists I know and love are those who attended retreats I facilitated. Many are writers I was introduced to through the magical six degrees of separation that link us all. Some fellow writers I have never physically met have become e-mail buddies. Others became friends when we appeared at the same speaking venues or conferences. Some are writers who share the same publisher, agent, or editor. And of course there are the people at my publisher who work with me to put the book out. Those I have come to know over time, in addition to my family and my close friends, form a consistent community of support for my writing process. The support they offer is based on their knowledge of what I need in order to take the creative process deeper. My friends, colleagues, and agent know that I do not need to hear that I should be more disciplined, should work faster or harder. They ask about the "secret Oriah deadline," knowing I like to leave myself plenty of time for rewrites. They encourage me to take time off, to slow down and enjoy my family and the forest around me, knowing that these are things that feed me and my creative work as surely as a disciplined writing schedule, and knowing also that these are things I am likely to neglect.

Gradually, over time, as you cultivate your commitment to doing your creative work, strengthen your willingness to begin, continue, deepen, and put your work out into the world, you will meet others who become part of your community of support. If you want to know if you are headed in the right direction, if you are cultivating a life that supports you in developing your creative work, take a look around and see where you are spending the life you have been given. Is a consistent and substantial part of your energy—your time, space, energy, and money—spent on your creative work? Does the way you've choreographed your life—the people with whom you are intimate, the way you relate to the broader community, the look, use, feel, and location of your home, the things you do for recreation, the way you provide for yourself and those who depend upon you—support you in your creative work? How many of your choices—in what you read, where you go for vacations, what you watch on television or at the movies, how you care for your physical well-being—feed you in a way that enables you to do your creative work? Do you regularly provide for yourself a way to come to stillness, a way to touch that which is larger than you no matter what you call it, a way to come into relationship with the mystery? Ultimately our creative impulse is fed by and connected to a creative life force we cannot name, and our creative expression is sustained only when we cultivate, each in our own way, an awareness of the vast sacredness in which we participate with every breath.

The artist's life is simply an ordinary human life that is consciously choreographed to support ongoing creativity in both you and those around you. The more your choices are colored and shaped by this commitment, the more you will find yourself in the places where you will meet others who share this commitment. And you will recognize each other, and see yourself in another, and create for yourself a community of the heart.

FOR CONTEMPLATION

- What if there are two critical aspects to cultivating a life that supports and encourages the creative work you want to do: an honest assessment of your own strengths and weaknesses; and the creation of a community of support? Do you know yourself? Do you have a community of support?

LIVING THE ARTIST'S LIFE

- Do you have time alone? Find a way to spend regular time in solitude, alone or at least away from those you know. Use the time that is available (on the commuter train, walking to school or work, etc.) to be fully present with yourself, to simply notice without judgment the way you respond to the world around you.

- Assess the balance of fertile empty time and disciplined focus in your life. If you are not doing the creative work you ache to do, you may need to increase one or the other of these two necessary elements. Be honest with yourself. Do you procrastinate frequently, or do you fill available time with too much focused activity? Which people, places, and practices help you find the mix of diligent practice and letting go that supports you in doing your creative work? Experiment. Reassess. Make changes.

- Look at where you spend your resources—time, energy, money. Are these expenditures in areas that support your creative endeavors?

- Take a look at your choices—the people with whom you spend time, the way you relate to the broader community, the look, use, feel, and location of your home, the things you do for recreation, the way you provide for yourself and those who depend upon you. Do all of these support you in your creative work?

- Assume that the people who love you want you to be happy. If you feel they are not supporting you in your efforts to do creative work, let them know how important that work is to you. Tell them how they can support you. Ask for their support.

- Do not expect your family to be the sole provider of encouragement and support for your creative work. Seek out others similarly involved in or enthusiastic about creative work. Remember: your credential for participating in the desired mutual support is that you are doing your own creative work.

- If you are going to enroll in a class, ask questions of the teacher beforehand about how the course is designed. Consider your needs. Do you need more time to do your creative work, more feedback on your work, ideas to stimulate the work, the company of those similarly involved, or something else? Determine if this is the course for you. If you start the class and find you are doing less of your creative work, quit the class!

WRITING EXERCISES

- Imagine holding in your hand something that is very pre-cious to you (if the item is accessible, actually hold it in your hand). Write about what comes to you as you hold this item.

- Write about one of your body parts and relate it to a body part of a relative from a previous generation. Who do you see from your family in your body? Begin with

     I have my _____ (mother's, father's, uncle's . . .) _____ (eyes, ears, nose etc.)

- Describe the body part, how you feel about it, what it says about you and your family and let the writing go where it will.

- Write a personal ad seeking

     —a partner, lover, friend, or soul mate

     —a home

     —work that will feed the body and soul

     —the muse

Be specific. What do you want? Be seductive. What do you offer?

eleven

BEING RECEIVED

R honda, the instructor, walks slowly around the table, a stack of manuscripts held to her chest. She pauses and smiles slightly, glancing my way. My stomach turns over. It is not a warm smile. Rhonda is in her early forties, a short solid woman with large round glasses that give her a deceptively wide-eyed look. The group seated around the table, ten men and women gathered here on the first day of a two-week residential writing retreat, are silent and waiting. Suddenly she throws a single manuscript onto the center of the table. We all jump.

"Nothing," she says with a sneer, "says amateur like single spacing!"

Despite the fact that there is more red ink than black on the paper and half of that single-spaced first page has a bold red *X* marked through it, I recognize it as my manuscript. It is my account of the day my friend Catherine had a brain aneurysm burst while she was at my home. It is my story of taking her to the hospital, of holding on to her when she stopped breathing, of trying to save her, of struggling not to give in to the overwhelming urge to scream.

I don't want to scream now. I just want to disappear. But the fun is just beginning. It is 1994, and this is the first writing workshop I have ever attended. As requested, I had sent in a ten-page manuscript with my admission application. The instructions had not specified double spacing. But apparently the format of my manuscript is the least of my problems. In both private sessions and group meetings, Rhonda repeatedly reviews the extensive evidence that I am simply someone who will never write anything worth reading. Her comments are punctuated with hopeless shrugs and sighs. Apparently my "writing voice" is not one that a reader would ever trust, I include too many details in my narration, the story (despite being true) is not believable, and my account of inner responses to external events is "too sentimental."

As group members are given copies of each other's manuscripts and asked to join in the critique, they take their cue from Rhonda. The sessions become a bloodbath, with group members offering often inarticulate and sometimes irrelevant but always harsh commentary. In all fairness to the group, this does seem to be the expected mode of participation. Many of those with previous writing group experience seem familiar with this bloodletting approach. No one appears to find it odd or objectionable. Confused, I try to keep my head down and consider it a minor accomplishment to get through the two weeks without being counted among those reduced to tears. Rhonda is, after all, the Published Author. After writing a book on surviving a life-threatening illness, she, according to her promotional materials, developed an interest in facilitating workshops that offer the healing power of writing true stories. Throughout the workshop Rhonda's slash-and-burn approach to critiquing writing is applied more or less uniformly to all the manuscripts, although several group members and a couple of the staff working at the college where the seminar is taking place surreptitiously comment that she does seem to have particular enthusiasm for ripping my writing apart. Perhaps I remind her of a sister she resents, a colleague she feels was unfairly promoted, a teacher who once harshly criticized her work. There is no way to know. I remind myself not to take it personally, but I can feel my desire to write and my hopes of writing well dwindling fast.

Then, one afternoon in the second week, we are offered a reprieve from the relentless sessions of criticism. Rhonda has invited a magazine writer from New York to come and speak to us. We are treated to a three-hour lecture on how there is simply no point in writing for magazines: the competition is fierce, the pay is lousy, the market is shrinking, and even well-known authors are quitting in droves to become brain surgeons or taxi drivers.

It is only much later that I realize what I should have done. I should have left. Perhaps there were people in that workshop who found Rhonda's method spurred them on to write more. Certainly some of her criticisms were valid. I had included too many details in my story, and my descriptions of emotional responses were not skillfully done. But her delivery did not seem intended to guide, encourage, and correct but rather to dissuade group members from writing at all. By the end of the workshop more than half the participants told me privately that they were going to give up writing altogether. Most were quietly resigned. Several were explicitly grateful for what they saw as honest feedback that had saved them from wasting their lives doing something they were now convinced they would simply never be able to do well.

This group and the facilitator's method may have been particularly harsh. I don't know. I never participated in another group where I was not either in charge or helping to set the ground rules. Certainly I have heard enough stories of other people's experiences in courses—writing, art, music, and drama—to know that Rhonda's method, while perhaps not the rule, is by no means the exception. What I did learn is that the process of offering our work to others, of having our work received, is one that needs to be consciously considered, prepared for, and handled with care if it is to enhance and further our creative work.

Because creative work does need to be received. It's part of the process of creation to be seen. That process by which you as the writer or artist or composer draw upon the raw materials around you and make something more, that act of creation by which you dip into the sea of potentiality and collapse infinite possibilities into a singularity, is repeated in a similar and yet different way each time another person receives the piece you created. If Buber is right and we do in fact engage with the Other, with a *Thou*, a form, an archetype from the collective unconscious or the realm of the gods that is seeking manifestation and relationship to the world through what we create, surely that relationship is not intended for us alone. Having the results of our work received is as critical to the process as is any of the other stages of creative work. Without this we cannot move on to new work, or we do so carrying the weight of what is incomplete, what is yet to be received.

Of course, Buber called the one receiving the work the *receptive beholder.* Rhonda was not very receptive, and she seemed to have an assassin's understanding of what it means to behold. Offering our work to others puts us in a vulnerable position, although there are settings where we can create boundaries that reduce the risk of real damage being done. In the groups I have facilitated, feedback is limited to what is asked for and is deliberately gentle with first drafts. My experience is that this works not only to encourage more writing (which will lead to better writing) but also to gently push us in the direction of more powerful writing. When we hear what works, what touches people, the ineffective work falls away and the powerful work grows deeper, gets better. When we want more particular feedback, we need to seek out those we trust, those who have skills related to the work we are trying to do as well as the ability to communicate suggestions with gentle honesty and skillful directness, ways that do not imply that we are morally lacking for our creative choices or that there is only one way to create a desired result.

But most of the time we have little or no control over how our work is received. When we dare to share in a public way what we have created, we are exposed to the opinions, comments, and questions of both those we know and love and total strangers, some of whom have limited interest in the work or minimal communication skills. This vulnerability may make us hesitant to put our work into the world. And, given the competition for and odds against publication or distribution, all we really have to do is sit back and wait to be "discovered" if we want to ensure that our work stays within the safety of the private realm. But it's not about putting *my* work out into the world. It's about finding a way for the work to be received. It's about acknowledging that the work itself needs to be received if it is to be complete and that we need to have it received if we are to move on in our own creative endeavors.

There are a thousand ways to have your creative work received. Before anything of mine was published, four times a year I mailed out a newsletter filled with bits of my writing to those who had come to study with me, to friends and family, to pretty much anyone who was willing to give me their postal address. At the same time, I placed small ads in local magazines advertising classes on the spiritual practices I had been learning. These classes and groups met first in my home and then, when the numbers grew large enough, in rented halls. At these events I often read from my writing and recited my poetry. Most of the time I did not ask for feedback. I was not looking for praise or critique. I figured people could vote with their feet. If what I shared did not offer anything of value to others, the room would be empty the following week. Thankfully, people came back.

Countless men and women have figured out ways to have their creative work received. Canadian humorist and storyteller Sandra Shamas laughingly talks about renting a hall, putting up posters, and doing her first monologue in Toronto because she simply didn't know that you weren't supposed to do it this way, that you were supposed to wait for a producer to come forward, offer you money, and orchestrate the whole production. Musician and songwriter Loreena McKennitt produced her own CDs and sold them on street corners while playing her harp and singing for the passing crowd for years before she was offered a recording contract and indoor concert venues. Diana Meredith, a dear friend and gifted artist, put together an exhibit of her paintings last year so that friends and strangers could receive her work and celebrate its beauty. My husband, Jeff, showed his photographs and slides at a local art gallery, accompanying the images by playing his own compositions on the piano. I have met many talented musicians, composers, artists, and writers who have found ways to have their work received. Sometimes this simply means arranging for friends and family to gather for an evening of readings or music. Sometimes it means creating a Web site where the work can be accessed by both friends and strangers who stumble upon it. Usually these offerings do not bring fame or fortune, but most of the time their authors figure out a way to come close to breaking even financially using limited sales and small contributions to pay for CD production, Web site maintenance, printing costs, or the rental of space. Advances in computer technology and the development of simple-to-use desktop publishing programs have increased the number of self-published books. Given the easy access to computer graphics and high-quality inexpensive printing, many of these books are indistinguishable from those produced by major publishing companies.

If you do creative work, you must figure out a way to have it received. You also need to consider how much of the labor you can or want to do and at what point you may need or want to enlist the help of others. Writing needs the eye of an outside editor. Performances need the eye of a director. And even if you have the skills to do all your own production, publicity, or distribution, you have to consider if you have the time and inclination. This is not meant to discourage you from putting your work out into the world on your own. Find out what is involved, assess your resources, and decide on a course of action that will work for you. If the point is to have your work received, what is the easiest way to do this? Is sharing writing on a Web site easier for you than convincing bookstores to carry your book, or do you want to do both? Do you know people who have the skills you need, and who may need your skills, with whom you can do an exchange? Connecting with community can make the process of having your work received much easier and more enjoyable. Seek out those who did it before—writers who self-published, performers who produced their own shows, musicians and composers who produced and sold their own CDs—and ask them to tell you what they learned, how they did it, who they know that might be helpful.

Some worry that sharing their work in small homegrown ways may make them vulnerable to having ideas stolen. Of course, there is always that risk. But refusing to share your work because you fear it will be expropriated will not enhance the flow of creativity you hope to tap into when working and may in fact bring the process to a complete halt. Be sensible. Copyright materials where appropriate and then share what you have. Try to keep a balance between honoring your contribution to the world and so wanting to be credited for your efforts and remaining aware that the work may have a life of its own far beyond your concerns. The unauthorized copying of my prose poem "The Invitation," which was technically a violation of copyright, and its distribution through the world via the Internet directly contributed to a publishing company's willingness to take a chance on an otherwise unknown author.

We all know that when we put our work out into the world, something might happen to take that work to a larger audience. Sandra Shamas's performances drew increasingly large crowds until someone did come along and offer to produce her shows. Some self-published books that have been sold out of the trunk of the author's car have caught the attention of publishing companies and led to six-figure advances. Sometimes offering what we have created, allowing our work to go out into the world, leads to recognition and resources that open our lives to undreamed-of opportunities to do our work and have it received by vast numbers of people. I do not want to diminish for one moment the blessings this can bring when it happens. But the often wonderful gifts and surprising challenges of any degree of fame and fortune that may come from our work going into the world are secondary consequences of something that is simply beyond our control. We can respond to rising book sales, be grateful, and try to wisely use the resources that come our way with increased visibility and income, but we cannot make these things happen, and we must not make them the focus or purpose of our creative work. If success in the world becomes our goal or preoccupation, if recognition and material gain become a primary motivation for doing the work, the creative work will suffer. When I write I do not think about whether or not what I am writing is marketable, timely, or something people will respond to positively. If I did, it would abort the process, would disconnect me from the center of both myself and the creative flow I seek. Years ago I read that Irish novelist James Joyce defined pornography as any creative work designed to elicit a specific desire, shaped to sell something. I remember thinking at the time that this was a harsh judgment, but now I wonder. We cannot design our creative work primarily to sell something—including the work itself—or we lose an essential aspect of both the process and the product, although we may sell our work after it is created in order to have the means to continue creating. Creative work, the process of creation, is not a means to an end. It is an end in itself, a way to go home.

I'm not inclined to wear T-shirts emblazoned with messages, but if I were, mine would read, Don't Settle for Success! Over and over I have heard in the voices, letters, and e-mails of gifted writers, published and unpublished, an almost desperate desire to have a best seller, to be invited to speak at large venues or appear on well-known television shows. Beneath the desire, in these thoughtful and talented people, to do good work and contribute to the world, there is often a quiet but desperate sense that it will all be for nothing if it does not lead to some level of fame and fortune. When I am asked by writers for tips on how to get a big publishing contract, how to raise their profile or increase their book sales, I want to tell them to simply forget about it. Focus on the work. Do the work. And then do it again. Make it better, deeper, richer. Stretch yourself in your creative work, and let something else take care of the marketing.

I am not advocating that you not take care of business. If you want to get published—and there are many advantages to having the resources of a publisher behind you—send your manuscript to agents and publishers, contact those you think might be helpful, and set aside a certain amount of time to make and mail packages of material and do follow-up phone calls. Having an agent is necessary to get most publishers or galleries to even look at your work, and an agent provides what at times can be a critical buffer between the creative work and the business aspects of having your work in the world. You don't get all the rejection slips or rave reviews mailed to you personally and can choose to never look at any of them. If you are published or your work is to be shown, you need to make yourself available for the aspects of marketing you can do as the creator to help support sales and distribution. Do interviews, visit bookstores, attend gallery openings and theater premiers, give talks, answer questions. But don't make marketing the focus of your life or material success the goal of your creative work. Treat these tasks like all the other logistical things that keep life and limb together, like doing laundry or paying your electric bill, like mowing the lawn or doing the dishes.

Bring your full attention to the task while you are doing it, and then put it out of your mind. Do what needs to be done to send your work out into the world with whatever opportunities are right in front of you, whether an international book tour or a reading at the open mike in your local pub, and let go of any attachment to having these actions bring about particular results.

In a culture that values material gain and worldly success, at a time when many are preoccupied with celebrity, this can be a lot harder than it sounds. And success in the world does not necessarily make it any easier. When *The Invitation* became an international best seller, many things in my life changed. For the first time in my life I was required to pay income taxes! I ditched my dilapidated twelve-year-old Hyundai Pony and bought a newer-model Honda. I was able to buy groceries without continuously adding up the total cost in my head as I went through the store to ensure I had enough money to pay at the checkout counter. More important, I put money aside so I would be free to do more writing in the future without worrying about how to pay the bills. I also found myself on the receiving end of a great deal of unfamiliar and sometimes seductive attention. People wanted me to speak at their conferences, sign at their bookstores, and do interviews on their radio and TV shows. And I was happy to oblige, grateful for the opportunity to talk about the things that matter most to me and to meet a wide variety of people.

But of course all this came along with other kinds of attention: strangely intimate and initially baffling messages from people I barely knew expressing a desperate desire to rekindle or deepen nonexistent friendships; the inexplicable disappearance of some people from my life, people who assumed without consulting me (and often could not be convinced otherwise when I did catch up with them) that I would no longer have the time or inclination to include in my life people like themselves, people who were not well known; countless e-mails and letters from readers who felt my writing had touched them. The whole thing was an unexpected roller-coaster ride, and I admit it took me a while to find my inner balance with all these responses to what was a very unexpected and modest level of success. I cannot imagine how people who are truly famous, particularly those who achieve fame at a young age, handle it.

As difficult as it sometimes was to deal with the reactions of others, it quickly became apparent that these were both beyond my control and most often more about others than they were about my writing or me. A man whose fiancée had broken off their engagement after reading *The Invitation* wrote to me begging me to stop writing, imploring me to "stop ruining people's lives" with my stories. I had no trouble discerning that my book could not possibly have been the cause of his breakup, and I was pretty sure that if he were mentally stable he would realize this when he resurfaced from the acute pain of loss. Several days later the young woman's parents e-mailed me a letter of gratitude. They felt that reading my book had helped their daughter break off her engagement to a man they feared was controlling and abusive. Just as my writing could not be blamed for the couple's breakup, neither could it be credited with saving the young woman from an abusive relationship.

When blame or credit come flying at you, it's hard to check the impulse to duck, hard to stand still and just let another's reaction be theirs and go right through you. But if you can stand still, if you can acknowledge what you are being given and any internal reaction you are having, pleasant or unpleasant, and let it move through you, you will be free to continue your creative work. At various speaking engagements over the years, several women told me about receiving my prose poem or one of my books just before or after the death of one of their children. I listened as they told me how they hung on to the words I had written in order to take their next breath, to live through the next day without their son or daughter. I could not imagine how any words would help in the face of such pain. I may have, on occasion, a moment of insight, but I know that if I sat down to deliberately write something I thought would comfort someone who has suffered the loss of her child, I would simply not know what to write. One day, listening to one of these stories of gratitude, and feeling myself pull away wanting to say, "It wasn't me," I finally got it. It's not about me! It's about what may happen for others when we do our small part, when we bring ourselves to our lives and our creative work as fully as we are able.

Although people can be deeply influenced, inspired, or guided by creative work—and it is everyone's hope that their work will speak to others and offer them something of value—each person is responsible for how they respond, for the meaning they create in their lives from the work we create. If we have been true to the work, have allowed ourselves to be fully engaged with the creative process, have been faithful to that strange invisible relationship with Buber's *Thou*, the receptive beholder of our work will have his or her own direct experience, own unique encounter with the divine life force that danced with us as we created. While I always find it fascinating to hear what others receive from this encounter, I know I cannot take blame or credit for it beyond the small satisfaction of knowing I brought all of myself to the process and held nothing back in the writing. The reactions to the worldly success of *The Invitation* that disturbed me most were my own. The rush of excitement and energy from constant requests to do speaking engagements and interviews ebbed away and left a strange and nameless fear when the number of e-mails and phone calls began to diminish slightly. Four positive professional reviews could be quickly outweighed by one less-than-enthused critique by a disappointed anonymous reader. I began to worry about writing the next book. What if I couldn't do it again? What if I wrote something truly horrible, revealing to the world that the success of *The Invitation* was just some kind of fluke, a one-shot wonder?

Eventually the attention calmed down and so did I. In many ways success is a fluke. It's important to remember when we are feeling good about material success or depressed by sales figures that mean we have to teach another course or take on another shift of driving a cab to pay the bills that there are countless brilliantly conceived and beautifully written books that have been sold off in remainder bins for less than the cost of what it took to print them. And there are some best sellers that make you wonder. I only have to look around to know this truth: *material success is not a reliable barometer of the worth of creative ideas or work.*

The opinions of others offered after a piece of work is completed and out in the world are not particularly useful. I once heard actress Meg Ryan say that she simply did not read reviews of the movies she had been in. I don't know where I got the idea that I was obligated to read reviews, but Ms. Ryan's comment liberated me. If you can't help but be affected by reviews—and I am the first to admit that despite my best intentions I am deeply affected—don't read them! I stopped reading reviews and asked others not to send me any more, no matter how positive. I had never really paid much attention to sales figures, so I simply consciously increased my resolve not to look in that direction, to simply receive whatever came with gratitude.

After being distracted for a short time, I learned to keep my eye on the ball—my ball—which for me is writing. I stopped automatically accepting all invitations for speaking engagements and considered how many I could do and stay healthy and keep doing my creative work. I considered venues that intrigued or drew me regardless of anticipated numbers or the voices of well-meaning program directors urging me to "strike while the iron is hot." I continued to do what truly serves the writing, and a certain amount of book touring and publicity gives me the pleasure of meeting readers and the opportunity to support bookstore owners while helping to ensure the book sales that will allow me to continue to write with ease in the future. What is important to remember is that sales are just one way of having your work received, a way that can be a means to the end of continuing to do your creative work, not vice versa. Otherwise you risk allowing the tail to wag the dog. The only guide in determining if you are on track or off is the willingness to continuously and honestly examine what really serves your creative process.

Recently at one bookstore appearance, weary of being described in the language of marketing as a "visionary author," I told the woman preparing to introduce me to forget the biography my publicist had sent her, to simply focus on the book I was there to talk about. "You know," I said, "it's never really about the singer. It's always about the song."

She smiled and replied, "But people come to see you. They want to know the woman who wrote the book." I reluctantly accept that in this culture the marketing of creative work includes, to some extent, the marketing of the authors of that work. But I'm pretty sure that believing your own publicity, beginning to think of oneself as a Visionary Author, would not serve the creative process. And whatever does not serve the creative process—a frenetic pace, an attachment to achieving fame and fortune, a preoccupation with how others see you or your work—has to be left by the wayside.

When we put our creative work into the world we sometimes feel as if a piece of ourselves is exposed to potential rejection or acceptance, praise or ridicule. But we are wrong. As important as our work is, we are not the work we create. If we can keep and cultivate this perspective, we will be less likely to become attached to achieving material success, to having our work acknowledged or received in a particular way. I take it as a necessary and positive part of the process that I feel a deep sense of attachment to the work I am currently doing. Often the feeling is akin to the early stages of being in love. The line where I end and the other—the work—begins feels hazy and, for a time, indistinguishable. The work I have created often feels like a beloved child. But when the time comes to let the work be received, I need to let it go and let it make its own way in the world. I do a small ceremony to help me do this. Each time a new book is released, I carry one signed copy around in my knapsack and leave it at some random location. The first book I wrote was left in the low branches of a tree in a park near my home in Toronto, wrapped in a silk scarf. When I returned a week later to see if it was gone, I passed the spot just as a man was unwrapping the book and sitting down on a park bench to look at it. I watched from a distance as he read parts of the book. About an hour later he carefully wrapped the book up and placed it back in the tree. A week later the book was gone, and I wondered how many people had taken it down and placed it once again in the tree before someone finally took it home. Later books have been left at airport lounges, government offices, and bus stops. And each time I leave a copy of the book in this way I do a prayer that it might find its way into the hands of someone for whom it will have meaning. As I pray I imagine cutting an imaginary umbilical cord between myself and the book, releasing it into the world and consciously giving away all attachment to where it goes or how it travels.

In July of 2001 I saw a television interview with actor Martin Sheen. In it he said, "I'm not asked to be successful. I'm asked to be faithful . . . to myself."

As writers, artists, dancers, or composers, as people who engage in creative work, we are not asked to be successful in the world. Success may come or it may not. And if it comes it, like all else, will pass. We are not asked to be successful. We are asked to be faithful. This is what the work requires, a commitment to be faithful to ourselves, to the process, to the truth we touch and the creative impulse that seeks expression. To be faithful to the process, we have to allow the work to be received, and we have to know ourselves well enough to discover ways of doing this without being pulled off center and away from the work by promises of approval or material success. We must be faithful—full of faith that the process of creating will be enough to feed us and the world.

FOR CONTEMPLATION

- What if all creative work, to be complete, needs to be received?

- What if material success really is not any kind of barometer of the worth of creative ideas or work?

HAVING WORK RECEIVED

- Don't make marketing the focus of your life or material success the goal of your creative work. When you are doing your creative work, forget about sending it out into the world.

- Brainstorm with friends and family about ways to have your creative work received. Make a list of possibilities and keep adding to it.

- For each viable idea on the list, consider the tasks involved, your skills and inclinations, and the resources available. Which possibility appeals to you most as a way to have your work received? Which possibility would be the easiest to pursue?

- Consider: Is there something you are unconsciously waiting for someone else to do in order to have your work received? Can you do it yourself? Are there others who would help that you need to ask for assistance?

- Seek out others who have offered their work by the means you are considering. Ask them to give you their advice, to tell you what they learned. Listen and learn from their mistakes and successes.

- Wherever possible and without too much angst, copyright your material before sharing it. Put a copy or photograph of the work in a sealed envelope and mail it to yourself. Put the unopened envelope in a safe place (the postmark establishes when the work was completed).

- Take care of business. If you want to, send your work to those you think might be helpful: agents, publisher, marketing people, etc. Set aside a regular but limited amount of time to do this, and then forget about it. Keep doing your creative work.

- If your work should receive attention and remuneration, say, "Thank you," and keep doing your creative work.

- Consider not reading reviews, positive or negative, of work that has been completed.

- If you are in a situation in which others tell you how your work affected them, positively or negatively, don't take it personally. Stand still as they tell you their story, and receive them fully. Smile, say, "Thank you," walk away, and keep doing your creative work.

- Consider that others' responses to your work are as much or more about them than about the work.

- Consider that as important as your creative work is to you, you are not your work. Therefore, others' responses to the work are about their experience of the work, not their experience of you.

- Devise a small personal ceremony for releasing the work a short while after it is in its completed form. Keep it simple (leave a copy in a public place, send copies anonymously to a charitable organization), but include the intent of offering what you have created to the world and letting go of being attached to how it is received.

WRITING EXERCISES

- Begin a story with the sentence,

  Suddenly I realized it was going to be a completely different day from the one I had planned.

- Complete each phrase repeatedly:

  I don't know . . .

  I don't know how . . .

  I don't know if . . .

- Write the truest statement you can about any or all of the following:

  love

  God

  chairs

  fear

  grief

your ambitions

what you ache for

cabbages

sex

violence

work

play

aluminum siding

monogamy

good china

bliss

home

silence

- Then, after each of these statements, complete the phrase,

  If this is not true . . .

twelve

ENDINGS

W hen I read a book I am enjoying, one in which I feel immersed in the words on the page, I read at high speed, gobbling up stories or ideas, characters or insights like a good meal served after a long fast. But as I near the end of the book, as I become aware that there are only a few chapters remaining, I begin to slow down. I am both anxious to know how it ends and reluctant to finish. I want to make the journey last so I do not find myself pulled too soon out of the world the author has created.

I experience something similar when I am writing: an eagerness for completion combined with a reluctance to have the process end. Seeing the end in sight, beginning to write the final chapter, I am exhilarated to see that the process I began many months earlier, a process that has included moments of doubt about whether or not any satisfactory completion would ever be achieved, is now almost over. But I also find within myself a reluctance to come to the end, a desire to prolong the rhythm and

intensity of writing for many hours each day. Suddenly, just before the end, I find myself slowing down, allowing household
tasks or business details I would normally set aside to distract me.

At the end of any particular project of creative expression, we
are faced with a number of daunting questions, not the least of
which is, *Now what?* After months, possibly years, of having your
choices about where to spend at least part of your time, energy,
and attention shaped by a particular piece of creative work, what
will you do when the project is complete? Recently a writer ad-
mitted to me that her constant and grueling writing schedule allowed her to postpone indefinitely dealing with other areas of her
life in which she knows she needs to make some changes. If we
have been using our creative work to avoid other areas of our
lives, we may not be overeager to complete work on a project,
may be all too aware of the people or situations that need our attention or are awaiting wisdom we are not sure we have. And if
you don't have a publisher waiting for the manuscript, a gallery
hoping to show your work, or a producer wanting to launch your
CD, reluctance to bring the work to completion may be fueled by
not knowing how to go about sharing it with others or fears that
your work will not be well received. All these concerns and the
sometimes vague but very real anticipation of the inevitable loss
that comes with all endings can combine to make us hesitate to
bring the work to completion. When we are deeply involved in
the creative process, an intimacy between ourselves and the work
develops, an intimacy we may not want to give up, unsure of our
ability to journey there again. When I am writing I become
steeped in the writing process. My dreams and thoughts are satu-
rated with images and ideas that relate to what I wrote today or
where I think the writing might take me tomorrow. I find myself

reluctant to live without the intensity that comes when I am fully engaged in creative work.

Sometimes we short-circuit the creative process because we become attached to the outcome, focused on making sure that we produce the book or song or image we had in mind when we began, refusing to let the process take us where it will. But we can similarly subvert the creative flow by becoming enamored with and attached to the process itself, by refusing to let a particular expression come to completion, by our reluctance to let the process end. Of course there are a number of endings within any given project: the end of a day's work, the end of a chapter or story or scene, the end of the rough draft or first rewrite. We can use all of these to hone our skill at recognizing when a point of completion has been reached, to practice letting go and moving on. As with all other stages of creative work, the time just before we have reached the end requires that we stay conscious of those inner voices or outer circumstances that could derail the process and, seeing and acknowledging them, keep right on working.

I stop when I have written all I have to write about a certain subject, when the story is complete. How do I recognize this? There is simply in this moment no more to say, nothing that needs to be added. I find myself reviewing my notes, rereading chapters, and writing things that have already been said more skillfully or placed more appropriately elsewhere in the book. The container, the book or story or poem, is full.

Sometimes the end comes because another kind of container, the time available for working on a particular piece or project—the ten minutes agreed to for a warm-up, the year set aside to write a book—is over. For some, deadlines feel like a threat to the creative process, an arbitrary cutoff point that has little or no regard for the process itself. But a deadline, whether one established by mutual agreement with others or one you set for yourself, can provide a useful container, a way of helping you focus on and distill the work at hand. To create is to make choices, which means sacrificing infinite possibilities. Sometimes the reality of limited time enables us to make those necessary choices when we are reluctant to do so, when we have become attached to keeping all our options open. Deadlines can be particularly useful as we gain experience in gauging how much creative work we can do in a given period of time and how long the whole process, including time for disciplined work and for sitting in empty moments seeking inspiration and direction, will take. When we develop our ability to set or agree to realistic deadlines, time becomes not the enemy but the ally, one of the many elements that help shape and create our work. Creative work, no matter how much it is connected to the stuff of dreams and unseen worlds, happens in and uses the realities of the material world in which we live. This is one of the ways in which it is not separable from our sexuality, our lives as physical beings who live with constant change and limited time. Most of the agreements we make that allow us to share our work with others involve timing.

I see time as an idea that helps me discern what is important and what is to be left behind, both in my life and in my creative work. I like to allow for what I hope will be extra time in setting deadlines so that when the unexpected happens—when my son requires extra assistance because of a broken leg or my computer crashes— I will not feel pressured to write under adverse conditions. This habit probably comes from the years when I had chronic fatigue syndrome, an illness that often made it difficult to predict if I could fulfill commitments or carry out planned activities. But within the larger, generous container of agreed-to submission dates, I set deadlines for myself that allow me to feel the sides of that container we call a human life. This sense of my own mortality and limitations applies a steady but gentle pressure to my resolve to stay with the process, to make choices, to keep writing. I generally work out a rough schedule for the progress of the book, one that will bring me to completion well before the agreed-to deadline, and with some flexibility I generally stick to the schedule. Saying I am going to finish the book by a certain date but not having any sense when I should be a quarter or halfway through leaves me open to misjudging my progress early on and feeling the pressure of too little time near the end. And while a clear but flexible timeline helps me work steadily, too much pressure robs the process of the joy that brings me to writing.

This works for me, and while you may need to find a different way of relating to deadlines, I urge you to find some way to use an awareness of the finite time we are given each day to inspire you to do more of the creative work you long to do. I know those who agree to share creative work with fellow artists, performers, or writers on a regular basis in order to create regular deadlines that inspire them to keep working. I do not know of anyone who has produced creative work without some inner or outer deadline to which they adhere.

While the work may be scheduled in time, the awareness that something is truly complete, like the writing itself, happens only in the present moment. As I come to the end, it is only in the present moment that I realize when I have said all I can say, have given all I have to give to a wholeness that has been created. In this sense the completion of a piece of creative work, when it comes, can often feel like a bit of a surprise. Of course, in the future I may have other thoughts on what I have written, may remember, imagine, or live new stories that relate to the themes of a particular book I have written. And those pieces may be included in another piece of writing, in a book or story or poem I write in another present moment. But for now, this is complete. And complete is good. Being prone to perfectionism, I try to remember the story about the creation of the world from the book of Genesis in the Old Testament. According to that story, God, having made the world, looked at what had been created and declared that it was good. Good is not perfect. Good is whole and complete. Good is enough because it serves life within and around us. Perfection does not serve life, does not serve the creative process, does not allow us to recognize when the process is complete.

And now what? Well, on the seventh day, as the story goes, after the work of creation was complete, God rested. What has been emptied must be refilled. If my own small creation, a book, is complete, it is because I have poured what I had to give—all of it—into its pages. I am spent. And as much as one part of me is reluctant to come to the end of a particular piece of creative work, another aspect of my self has been thinking about how nice it would be to take a few weeks off, to write in my journal without any thought for how what comes relates to a bigger whole or particular project. I am anticipating taking a holiday or catching up with friends and family who have seen too little of me in recent months.

I will tell you here what I know about how best to handle the time right after "The End," but you should probably know that rest is not my forte, and rest that rejuvenates is probably what we all need shortly after the end of a creative project. The first few times I completed a book, sent off the final rewrites, and waited to see what the cover design would look like, I simply did not know what to do with myself. I felt vaguely let down and had a strange sense of being suspended in time and space, unsure of how to proceed. I thought I would take a break, but after months of getting up early and diving into the writing each day, I was like a parked car whose motor keeps running, an engine that coughs and sputters even after the key is out of the ignition. The book may have come to completion, but the energy that had carried me through weeks or months of consistent writing had not instantly stopped, and I wasn't sure what to do now that the writing was finished. I was simultaneously tired and exhilarated, at once both ready to lie down and unable to really rest as my body and mind surged forward each day prepared to continue the momentum that I had maintained for months.

What I discovered works for me is to spend the month after a book is completed catching up on mundane business details, balancing the bankbook, updating the mailing list, straightening out contracts, and making logistical arrangements for future speaking engagements. These are tasks that occupy but do not require too much of my mind, tasks that I can do with decreasing speed as I begin to slow down. The best time for me to take a vacation, a trip to a place where I can simply sleep and read and eat food someone else has prepared, is about one month after the date of completion, the point at which I have mentally and physically slowed down enough to feel the deep fatigue that comes from sustained work. Of course, I have learned this, like most things, by trial and error, have spent holidays that were planned too soon unable to slow down and found myself, five weeks after completing a book, when I'd made new plans and commitments, collapsing with the need to sit still and do absolutely nothing.

During the month after the writing is completed, while I busy myself with catching up on household and business details that often have been neglected during the previous months of writing, I usually remain mentally very much with the finished book. One of the reasons why this is not a good time to take a holiday is that thoughts and questions about your creative work are bound to preoccupy you, making any real rest elusive. Anticipating sharing the work, you begin, hopefully for the first time, to consider how others, particularly close friends and family members, may react to parts they have not heard before, to ideas they might find offensive or objectionable. Because I often tell true stories about my own life, family, and community, it is inevitable that those who were involved in or close to the events have their own reactions, their own feelings about my version of the story and whether or not it should be included in creative work that is going to be publicly shared.

I can honestly say I do not consider these issues when I am writing. To do so, to concern myself with how others will react to what I am writing when I am trying to find and ride the creative flow of ideas and stories, would stop the process or shape it in a way that would make the writing ring false. When my first book was about to be published, a friend who had read the manuscript asked me how I had gotten around worrying about the reactions my parents or sons would have to such an honest account of some of the more intimate aspects of my life. Until asked, I had not even considered it. In a later book it felt important to include the story of my friend Catherine's brain aneurysm. My experience of being with her when the aneurysm burst and throughout her coma and struggle to recover opened me to the voice of longing so central to the book. I did give both Catherine and her husband, Roger, copies of those portions of the manuscript that detailed the story as I remembered and experienced it. Both of them gave me their blessing and their written permission to include the story in my book. Not surprisingly, Roger commented at the time that there were aspects of the story that he had experienced or remembered differently than I had, but he graciously acknowledged that since I was the author of the book, the rendition of the story presented had to be my own.

Telling true stories can be a tricky business. Memories are selective and subjective, and our motives are not always transparent even to ourselves. One woman I know, taking a class for writing memoirs, has been plagued by daily phone messages from her mother, who is terrified that her daughter will reveal something about the family that she feels certain should not be put down on paper, let alone shared with others. Often the limitations of time or space, our inclination or our lack of an infallible memory, may lead us to leave out of a story factual details someone else thinks are critical. But as the authors of creative work, we are the ones who make these choices; this is the responsibility we assume when we create. Although I lean in the direction of fidelity to fact, to the degree such a thing is possible (and my sons would be happy to tell you their renditions of stories I have written that they feel are incomplete or skewed in some way), I do think on occasion of my dear friend, filmmaker Mickey Lemle, and his directive to "never let a few facts get in the way of the truth or a good story."

Each of us has to consider how what we have created will affect those who receive the finished work, preferably after we have completed but before we have shared that work. This is part of the process of deciding what and how to share with the world.

When I have stopped writing, I consider certain questions in that brief window of time when, if I chose to, I could remove or change things. I ask myself, *Will anything I have written do harm to another? Have I been faithful to the truth as I know it? Is there anything I have held back or left out to make myself look better or because I cannot be with what is?* In sitting with these questions, I am not seeking definitive answers or second-guessing my choices. I am acknowledging and deepening my sense of responsibility for the choices I have made in doing and sharing my creative work.

You can see why the first month after completing a piece of creative work may not be the best time to try to take a holiday. And when it is time to take a break, each of us must discover for ourselves what will help us replenish. The rest needed after expending a great deal of time and energy on creative work should give us time to be very still, time preferably to sleep as long and as often as we need to, time to find and follow the deepest impulses of the body, which knows what it needs for health and balance. The time of rest also needs to offer us that which renews us at the deepest level of our soul, that which truly brings us joy. And joy is not about numbing out. Joy is ease with what is, being effortlessly present. For this reason, I continue to do my daily practice during my periods of rest, albeit often more slowly and usually later in the morning. My prayers, meditation, and journal writing help me find and follow what will provide what I need when a book is completed. Usually I am drawn to spend time in two places where I find rest and renewal: I go to the northern wilderness for silence and the song of the loon, to lay my cheek against the rough surface of a granite rock face, to remember that to which I belong; and I go to the city, to Toronto, to get my hair done and go to the theater, to shop, see friends, eat great food, and catch up on movies. I admit that I can take more than a week or two of the former and only about two to three days of the latter before I want to go home, but each has its place; each offers me a different but welcome form of rejuvenation.

If you have small children or a regular nine-to-five job, finding time to do your creative work may be such a challenge that finding additional resources to rest and renew after the work is completed may seem simply impossible. But my experience is that if you time it right, and if you give yourself completely to the process, time set aside to rejuvenate need not be long or involve much expense. When my children were younger I would simply declare certain days "bed days." Making meals in advance, I would rent some movies, pick up a couple of novels I had been waiting to read, take a long bath, and pull on a pair of comfortable pajamas. Ignoring the housework, I'd turn off the phone and run my household from my bed. A day spent like this, free of all guilt or any expectation of doing anything other than relaxing, can be as rejuvenating as a holiday that requires extensive time and energy to plan and implement. Sometimes, at the end of a particularly long period of intense work, I would take several of these days in a row, ordering pizza for dinner (much to my children's delight) and taking long naps in the daytime when they were at school.

However you find your way to it, if you want to continue to engage in the creative process, to write another book, compose another song, or make another piece of art, you will need to find ways to rest and return to the well to fill yourself with fresh energy and renewed inspiration, particularly when one project has been completed and before another is begun. Every ending provides the ground for a new beginning. Finding ways to rest and renew, we let ourselves lie fallow. And then, sometimes after what seems to be only a moment, sometimes after what feels like forever, you are caught by the glimpse of a new idea, another story or image or sound. And so you begin again. If we are faithful to our creative process, we do not need to worry that the completion of a particular expression of that process will bring an end to our participation in the life-giving flow of that work. Creation is ongoing, and the innate rewards of full and faithful participation will bring us back to the process over and over again.

When we create we come into relationship with what is infinite, unconditioned, and unchanging. Our spirituality is inseparable from our creativity. But we do our creative work by using those things—paint, stone, wood, plaster, words, ideas, sounds, movements—that are temporary, conditioned, and limited. Our creativity is inseparable from our sexuality, the sensuous physicality of being alive in the world. How we do this work—the choices we make to use a particular medium, to insert a phrase here, to capture the light there, to let the melody flow in a particular direction—mirrors who we are, an individuated piece of the divine life force, a soul. The impulse to create while dancing with the divine, to make something from materials that are conditioned and limited and so necessarily inadequate to do more than point in the direction of that which is unlimited and unconditioned, is what makes us human beings. I know the limitations of this process. The product of our work is only an approximation of what we receive when we create. Ironically, the spacious center of being that I touch when I write is beyond words. And still I feel compelled to write, to create something from that encounter. Our creative work is a mirror of what we are—a sacred marriage of that which is everlasting and infinite and that which is conditioned and temporary, a being in whom essence-awareness and ego-awareness can exist simultaneously when we are awake. Creative work allows us to fulfill our nature, and fulfilling our nature, we find what every human heart desires: peace and joy.

I have not always understood the essential nature of creative work. For years I doubted the value of following the impulse to write, wondered if a more purely "spiritual" path might not be more worthy, worried that my creative work was taking me away from deepening my spiritual practice. But always I am drawn back to writing. My personality has a propensity for perfectionism and a devotion to diligence, two qualities that could have led me to try to rise above the unavoidable limitations and foibles of one small human life. Writing saved me from the suffering this would have engendered, from the loss of joy this would have cost.

Creative work lets us touch the divine while rooting our lives in the soil of a human life, saves us from the temptation to move away from life within and around us. But I am drawn to write not because of my understanding about the nature of human beings, not even because of the spacious beingness I experience when I write. I write because I love words, because I love stories and poems and the beauty and meaning we can make from them in our lives. I am drawn to write not because I think the creative process will bring me happiness but because when I write I am happy. Paradoxically, when I write I am able to disappear, to get out of my own way and let life live through me, and I am able to show up completely, to be fully present with what is in this moment. When we are faithful to the process, when we allow ourselves to simultaneously disappear and show up fully, we do not leave the world behind for a more "spiritual" existence. We journey deeper into the world, deeper into the spirituality and sexuality of our human lives. Creative work does not offer us an escape, and it will not solve all that it is difficult in our lives or the world. But it does offer us a way to be with what is, to make meaning of our lives, to offer the world the life-sustaining beauty found at the heart of the truth creative work seeks to express. And it offers us a way to do this that brings us joy. It offers us stories that lift us when we are weary, images that stop us in our tracks when we are moving too quickly to savor the day we have been given, melodies of music and poetry that take our breath away and open us to what we ache for.

FOR CONTEMPLATION

- What if the limitations of time help us discern what matters and what does not, motivate us to make necessary choices in our creative work and in our lives?

- What if what is complete is good but not perfect? What if good is enough?

COMING TO "THE END"

- Consider your relationship to endings. Do you handle them well, deny them, race toward them, avoid them? Do you tend to leave things incomplete, or is it important to you to finish things you start?

- Find a relationship with deadlines that helps you do more creative work. As you gain experience, notice generally how much work you can do in any given period of time. Based on this, and on an awareness of the unpredictability of life and the creative process itself, set realistic deadlines, ones that allow enough time if unanticipated factors intervene while simultaneously providing you with the sense of a container that supports your commitment to continuing steadily. Make sure you include in your timeline opportunities for drastic changes in direction that necessitate starting over, for empty time and rest.

- Find out what makes you take deadlines seriously. Generally, agreements with others are helpful. If you don't have a formal agreement with a gallery or publisher or distributor, make agreements with others with whom you can share your work to deliver portions of it to them at a particular point in time. Intermediary deadlines for portions of a project can be helpful to establish pacing and avoid last-minute panic.

- Pay attention to the sense of completion—for a poem, a book, a painting, a film, a song—in the present moment. Ask, *Is this done? Is there anything else I need to add?*

- After the end of a piece of creative work, notice without judgment how you are feeling. Just be with whatever is there—elation, exhaustion, relief, nervousness, neutrality, fear.

- After a piece is completed but before it is shared with others, ask yourself some questions: *Will anything I have created do harm to another? Have I been faithful to the truth as I know it? Is there anything I have held back or left out to make myself look better or because I cannot be with what is?* Consider if you are willing to stand by what you have created, regardless of how others respond to the work or to you as its author.

- After the end, if you are still caught in the momentum, use the energy to catch up on the ordinary details of life. Clean your house, answer your mail, reacquaint yourself with your family, and plan some kind of break for the near future.

- A short time after the end, take a break. Consider what renews you and brings you joy. Consider what real self-care would look like given your needs and your resources. Schedule the break, and do the preparation needed to ensure it happens.

WRITING EXERCISES

- Describe an ending in your life, a moment when you knew something (a job, a relationship, your time in a particular home or geographical location, a way of being) was over, complete, finished.

- Complete the phrase,

  The last time I saw . . .

- Write a letter home from a dream vacation.

- Complete the phrase,

  Just when I thought it was over . . .

- Begin a story with the sentence,

  Before we go any further there is something you should know.

- Imagine you are at the end of your life, either about to die or in some kind of afterlife shortly after death. With the perspective of a life that has come to completion, answer the following questions with specific sensory details, allowing the writing to go where it will.

  What did you see?

  What were the best parts?

  What was the hardest part?

  How did you get through?

  What surprised you?

  What will you miss the most?

  What would you do differently if you could do it all again?

ACKNOWLEDGMENTS

All creative labors are made easier by the skills of attentive mid-
wives, and this book is no exception. I am grateful for the care,
guidance, and constant encouragement of my agent, Joe Durepos.
I offer my ongoing appreciation to the team at Harper San Fran-
cisco: for the coordinating efforts and creative ideas of Stephen
Hanselman, Mark Tauber, and Mickey Maudlin; the editorial
skills of John Loudon, Renee Sedliar, and Priscilla Stuckey; the
marketing skills of Margery Buchanan, Jennifer Johns, and Clau-
dia Boutote; the production and design abilities of Lisa Zuniga,
Terri Leonard, and Jim Warner. Many thanks for the enthusiasm
and hard work of publicist Adrienne Biggs.

My life and my creative work are enriched by the friends who
support me, often while they are doing their own creative work. I
hold in my heart Philomene Hoffman, Ingrid Szymkowiak, Judith
Edwards, Catherine Scoular, Linda Mulhall, Lise Tetrault, Liza
Parkinson, Peter Marmorek, Diana Meredith, Wilder Penfield,
Mark Kelso, Karen Drucker, Joan Borysenko, Elizabeth Lesser,

Gayle Straub, Jennifer Louden, Mickey Lemle, Harry Finberg, Thom Rutledge, and Daniel Ladinsky. Yours are the voices that keep me going.

To Joyce and Ken Beck and the staff of The Crossings in Austin, Texas—thanks for the great send-off. It made picking up my pen to begin again much easier.

My life has been blessed with a family that loves and supports me in my creative work. To my parents, Don and Carolyn House, and my sons, Brendan and Nathan, I send my deepest love and gratitude.

To Jeff—for all you put up with, for all your love, thank you.

And to that Sacred Mystery that is always with and around me, urging me to participate fully in this ongoing act of creation—I offer my life today and every day, with gratitude.

To receive information about Oriah Mountain Dreamer's schedule or publications, go to www.oriahmountaindreamer.com or write to

300 Coxwell Avenue
Box 22546
Toronto, ON
Canada
M4L 2A0

If you would like to find out more about the online writing circle mentioned in chapter 7, facilitated by Peter Marmorek, go to www.writerscroft.com.

DISCOVER THE WORLD OF
Oriah Mountain Dreamer
From HarperSanFrancisco

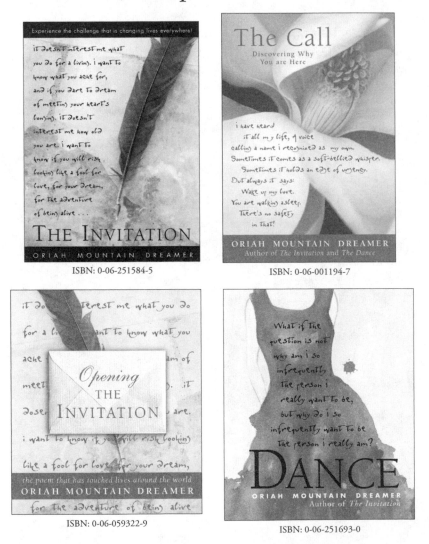

to legions of separation

successful~ faithful
the Journey